# Moralistics and Psychomoralistics

T0332372

This book brings together three distinct research programmes in moral psychology – Moral Foundations Theory, Cognitive Adaptations for Social Exchange, and the Linguistic Analogy in Moral Psychology – and shows that they can be combined to create a unified cognitive science of moral intuition.

The book assumes evolution has furnished the human mind with two types of judgement: intuitive and deliberative. Focusing on moral intuitions (understood as moral judgements that were not arrived at via a process of conscious deliberation), the book explores the origins of these intuitions, examines how they are produced, and explains why the moral intuitions of different humans differ.

Providing a unique synthesis of three separate established fields, this book presents a new research programme that will further our understanding of the various different intuitive moral judgements at the heart of some of the moral tensions within human society.

**Graham Wood** is Lecturer in Philosophy at the University of Tasmania, Australia. His research examines the relationship between human values and a scientific understanding of the human condition and draws on insights from moral philosophy, moral psychology, evolutionary psychology, and cognitive science.

# Routledge Focus on Philosophy

*Routledge Focus on Philosophy* is an exciting and innovative new series, capturing and disseminating some of the best and most exciting new research in philosophy in short book form. Peer reviewed and at a maximum of 50,000 words shorter than the typical research monograph, *Routledge Focus on Philosophy* titles are available in both ebook and print on demand format. Tackling big topics in a digestible format the series opens up important philosophical research for a wider audience, and as such is invaluable reading for the scholar, researcher and student seeking to keep their finger on the pulse of the discipline. The series also reflects the growing interdisciplinarity within philosophy and will be of interest to those in related disciplines across the humanities and social sciences.

**The Ethics of Undercover Policing**
*Christopher Nathan*

**Are Mental Disorders Brain Disorders?**
*Anneli Jefferson*

**Moral Choices for Our Future Selves**
An Empirical Theory of Prudential Perception and a
Moral Theory of Prudence
*Eleonora Viganò*

**Moralistics and Psychomoralistics**
A Unified Cognitive Science of Moral Intuition
*Graham Wood*

For more information about this series, please visit: www.routledge.
com/Routledge-Focus-on-Philosophy/book-series/RFP

# Moralistics and Psychomoralistics

## A Unified Cognitive Science of Moral Intuition

## Graham Wood

Routledge
Taylor & Francis Group

LONDON AND NEW YORK

First published 2023
by Routledge
4 Park Square, Milton Park, Abingdon, Oxon OX14 4RN

and by Routledge
605 Third Avenue, New York, NY 10158

*Routledge is an imprint of the Taylor & Francis Group, an informa business*

© 2023 Graham Wood

*British Library Cataloguing-in-Publication Data*
A catalogue record for this book is available from the British Library

ISBN: 9781032071725 (hbk)
ISBN: 9781032071718 (pbk)
ISBN: 9781003205746 (ebk)

DOI: 10.4324/9781003205746

Typeset in Times New Roman
by codeMantra

To my family and friends, because there is more to life than thinking about stuff.

# Contents

List of figures                                                              ix
List of tables                                                               xi
Preface                                                                     xiii
Author                                                                       xv

1   **The project and its theoretical framework**                             1
    *The elephant in the room   1*
    *The structure of the account   3*
    *What I mean by 'moral intuition'   3*
    *Evolutionary analysis   7*
    *Evolutionarily deep and distinct structures
        and processes   9*
    *Modularity and multi-level analysis of the mind   12*
    *Applying the 'tri-level' hypothesis from
        within cognitive science   15*
    *Drawing the linguistic analogy in moral psychology   17*
    *Moralistics and Psychomoralistics is the
        study of 'moral intuitions'   20*
    *One sense of normativity that is relevant to
        this project   22*
    *Summary of chapter   24*

2   **Unifying cognitive science of moral intuition**                        29
    *Sketching the elephant   29*
    *The Linguistic Analogy in Moral
        Psychology (LAMP)   31*
    *Moral Foundations Theory (MFT)   34*

*Cognitive Adaptations for Social Exchange (CASE)   36*
*A graphical representation of a combination*
  *of LAMP, MFT, and CASE   39*
*How this relates to work in social norms*
  *more broadly   41*
*Examples of moral intuitions at work   44*
*Summary of chapter   50*

3   **Introducing Moralistics and Psychomoralistics**                          55
*Introducing the elephant   55*
*The Linguistic Analogy in Moral*
  *Psychology as it has been drawn to date   55*
*Introducing some Moralistics and*
  *Psychomoralistics research questions   57*
*What is the moralistic equivalent to language?   58*
*Mords, mentences, and moral meaning:*
  *moral syntax and semantics   60*
*What is the moralistic equivalent of pragmatics?   65*
*Illustrating the re-framed linguistic analogy   68*
*Summary of chapter and a concluding remark   71*

*Index*                                                                          75

# Figures

1.1 The Müller-Lyer Illusion 13
2.1 The Principles and Parameters Model in Linguistics 39
2.2 The Principle and Parameters Model in LAMP 40
2.3 Unifying LAMP, MFT, and CASE in M&PM 40
3.1 Computation Generating Intuitions
Corresponding to Harman's Principle 70

# Tables

3.1 Questions Relating to Possible Analogues                58

3.2 Possible research questions in Moralistics and
Psychomoralistics                                           72

# Preface

I first started thinking about the larger themes that inform this book in 1990, when I wrote an essay called 'The Nature of Value? The Evolution of Value.' However, as is often the case in life, I then went on to other things. In 2000, I began a PhD and had planned to return to exploring these themes. But my PhD took a different direction, and it was not until 2009 that I had the opportunity to return explicitly to some of the themes explored in this book.

Study leave (sabbatical) from the University of Tasmania in 2011 allowed me to start thinking seriously about this project. In that year, I presented some of my ideas to academic audiences and discussed those ideas with individual researchers in the United Kingdom, United States, and Australia. Thank you to Steve Clarke, Neil Levy, and Julian Savulescu for making me welcome during my stay at Oxford, and Jeanette Kennett for making me welcome during my stay at Macquarie. Thanks to university research seminar audiences at Oxford, Boston, Duke, and Macquarie for listening to my ideas and offering thoughts. And thanks to Paul Bloom, Fiery Cushman, John Doris, Joshua Greene, Tamar Gendler, Deborah Kelemen, Thomas Nadelhoffer, and Walter Sinnott-Armstrong for discussions during my time in the United States.

The next chance I had for focused work on this project was in 2017 when, with the generous facilitation of my Head of School Tony Simoes da Silva, I was able to spend time at Exeter learning more about the linguistic analogy in moral psychology in discussion with Joseph Sweetman, my host at Exeter. Thank you, Tony, and Joseph, for making this possible, it was a very valuable time.

Outside these two distinct periods of time dedicated to thinking about this project, I have presented my ideas at a number of events in Australia. Thanks to all the audience members for offering comments. I have also had many useful and enjoyable conversations about my ideas over drinks, dinner, or walks, thanks to Dirk Baltzly, Steve Clarke, Philip Gerrans, Toby Handfield, Tony Kerr, Mike Kidd, Neil Levy, Ross Pain, Joel Stafford, and Stephen Stich. Thanks also to my colleagues in the School of Humanities, for their generosity in offering feedback that has helped improve my thinking and writing over the years, and to my colleagues in the university community more broadly, for making UTAS a great place to work.

After having had two decent chunks of time to think about this project, and given that my ideas were taking shape, I began looking for the best way to get my ideas into print. I submitted parts of this book to a number of journals, but without success. That said, I would like to thank the relevant journal editors and reviewers for reading my work and offering feedback. However, as this book demonstrates, I did succeed in getting this work published with the Routledge Focus series, perhaps because this series recognises the increasing interdisciplinarity of philosophy and perhaps because it is explicitly aimed at a wider audience.

Once I had a full draft manuscript, several people read it through from start to finish and offered valuable feedback. Thank you, James Chase, Chris Carney, Peter Davson-Galle, Peter Tranent, and Jason Whatley. I particularly offer my thanks to Peter Davson-Galle who read the manuscript through closely and offered very valuable and extensive comments, the book is a much better one as a result. I would also like to particularly thank my colleague James Chase, with whom I have had innumerable conversations over the years that have greatly helped me clarify my ideas. Thank you to the two anonymous Routledge reviewers, your comments were very helpful and have improved the quality of the book. Due to all these people's generous and constructive comments, the book has strengths it would otherwise not have. All the book's weaknesses remain, of course, my own responsibility! Finally, thanks to Lucy Batrouney at Routledge for offering me the chance to publish in the Routledge Focus series, and thanks to Sarah Pickles, Georgia Oman, Jenny Guildford, Kavya Shekar and the production teams at codeMantra and Routledge. The journey, started in 1990, has been long but interesting!

*Graham Wood*
*Launceston, Tasmania, 2022*

# Author

**Graham Wood** is Lecturer in Philosophy at the University of Tasmania, Australia. His research examines the relationship between human values and a scientific understanding of the human condition and draws on insights from moral philosophy, moral psychology, evolutionary psychology, and cognitive science. He is the author of 'On the perceived objectivity of some moral beliefs,' *Philosophical Psychology* 33 (1) 2020, pp. 23–41.

# 1 The project and its theoretical framework

## The elephant in the room

I see the rough outline of an elephant, and here I offer an account of what I see. This is, of course, a reference to the parable of five blind monks examining an elephant (Govier and Ayers 2012). Each monk is examining a different part of the elephant, so one understands the elephant as a trunk-like object, another understands the elephant as an ear-like object, etc. As I say, I only see a rough outline of this elephant. And as the elephant comes into clearer view in the future, no doubt, some things I say here will be discarded, but other things I say I hope will be retained. I understand the elephant as the systems and processes that produce moral intuitions in the human mind, and I call the study of the elephant, for want of a better name, Moralistics and Psychomoralistics: a unified cognitive science of moral intuition.

The five blind monks represent a number of current research programmes in moral psychology. Importantly, my use of the parable in no way implies any criticism of the currently existing research programmes. Great work is being done in these programmes. But, by the same token, I believe that the unification I offer here is valuable. And, if those who are currently pursuing the existing research programmes I seek to unify are not persuaded that there is an elephant, then at least I hope they take what I say here in the spirit of Mill's advice:

> the only way in which a human being can make some approach to knowing the whole of a subject, is by hearing what can be said about it by persons of every variety of opinion and studying all modes in which it can be looked at by every character of mind.
>
> (Mill 1991, 25)

DOI: 10.4324/9781003205746-1

At the very least, by bringing together the ideas I discuss in this book, I hope to contribute to humanity's understanding of the cognitive science of moral intuitions. In brief, here are the features of the elephant that I currently see. Humans use both deliberative moral reasoning and intuitive moral reasoning, and these two forms of reasoning are produced by distinct cognitive systems. Intuitive moral reasoning is produced by ancient biologically evolved systems. Given the rate of evolutionary change, there has been no significant change in the functioning of these biologically evolved systems throughout all human history. So, all recorded human moral codes, based on intuitive moral reasoning, should be understandable in terms of the functioning of these biologically evolved systems.[1] The process of intuitive moral reasoning categorises experience into morally relevant elements within morally relevant contexts. Some contexts are intuitively categorised as morally relevant, and others are not. Within morally relevant contexts morally relevant elements are recognised. Intuitive moral categorisation yields prescriptions such as 'impermissible' or 'obligatory' in relation to morally relevant elements within morally relevant contexts.[2] A number of current research programmes in moral psychology are all examining parts of the same intuitive moral categorisation system, including Moral Foundations Theory (Haidt and Joseph 2007), Cognitive Adaptations for Social Exchange (Cosmides and Tooby 1992), and the Linguistic Analogy in Moral Psychology (Mikhail 2011).

The linguistic analogy in moral psychology is particularly useful here because one can use a number of features of natural language (including words, grammatical sentences, and the meaning of grammatical sentences) to understand the way intuitive moral categorisation works. Morally relevant elements are analogues to words (I call them 'mords'). Morally relevant contexts are analogues to grammatical sentences (I call them 'mentences'). And, intuitive moral prescriptions, such as 'impermissible' or 'obligatory,' are analogues to the meaning of grammatical sentences. (I call this intuitive moral categorisation, or more simply, moral intuition.) Just as there are many natural languages, there are many moral languages. And, this is a major feature of the analogy. For example, according to the moral grammar of one moral language, 'justice intuitions' might always trump 'compassion intuitions,' while in the moral grammar of another moral language, 'compassion intuitions' might always trump 'justice intuitions,' or as is more likely, the grammar of the trumping relation might be more complex. But a major dis-analogy is that there are very few moral meanings. While the sentences in natural language mean many things. The mentences in moral languages mean very few things (e.g. mentences mean such things as 'impermissible' or 'obligatory,' or 'good' or 'bad'). The study of the cognitive systems that categorise experience into morally relevant elements in morally relevant contexts, including the resulting prescriptions (e.g. 'impermissible' or 'obligatory,' etc.), I call Moralistics and Psychomoralistics.

## The structure of the account

Here is how I will present my account. In the rest of this chapter, I set out the assumptions I am making in the pursuit of this unification. I won't argue for these assumptions, but I will present them, and discuss some of their implications. In Chapter 2, I explain, in broad terms, how a number of research programmes can be unified. I start by providing a reframing of the research programme known as the Linguistic Analogy in Moral Psychology (Rawls 1973; Dwyer 2007; Mikhail 2007; Dwyer, Huebner, and Hauser 2010). Then, I explain in general terms how two well-established research programmes can be incorporated into this reframed linguistic analogy. These are Moral Foundations Theory (Haidt and Joseph 2007; Graham et al. 2013, 2018), and work examining Cognitive Adaptations for Social Exchange within Evolutionary Psychology (Cosmides and Tooby 1992, 2008, 2015; Cosmides, Tooby, and Barkow 1992). Then, I explain how an emerging line of research developing a framework for a psychology of norms (Sripada and Stich 2007; Saunders 2009) can be incorporated. In Chapter 3, I present the detail of the reframed Linguistic Analogy in Moral Psychology. Some of what has been said in applying the linguistic analogy is on the right track and some is not. To distinguish my reframing of the linguistic analogy from what has been said to date, I introduce two terms Moralistics and Psychomoralistics, as names of two hopefully thriving research programmes of the future. These terms are simply adaptations of the terms 'Linguistics' and 'Psycholinguistics.'

So now I turn to the theoretical framework of the project. In the following, I will note a number of assumptions and offer some further associated preliminary remarks. I will not argue for the assumptions I present here, as that would be beyond the scope of this book. But, I take these assumptions to plausible in the context of evolutionary psychology.[3]

## What I mean by 'moral intuition'

The account I present here has a specific object of inquiry and I want to make it very clear what this project is about, and equally importantly what this project is not about. Perhaps, it is simplest to begin by stating what this project is not about. The word 'moral' in the book's title might imply that this book is concerned with justifying substantive moral claims in normative ethics, such as *justifying* the claim that slavery is impermissible. This book is not concerned directly with normative ethics. The word 'moral' in the title might also imply that this book is concerned with advancing a particular position in metaethics, such as the claim that it is *objectively* the case that slavery is impermissible. This book is not concerned with metaethics either. Both normative ethics (understood as answers to questions like 'How ought one live?') and metaethics (understood as inquiry into the nature and status of answers to normative ethical questions) are very interesting and important fields of inquiry, but this book will not engage directly with either. What I have to say in this book does have implications for both normative ethics and metaethics (that I may mention in passing), but I will not examine those implications in any detail here (simply because such an examination is well beyond the scope of this book). I will be seeking to understand moral intuitions, but in this book, I will be neither explicitly asserting or explicitly denying that these intuitions have what might be called 'moral authority' in a sense recognised by those who seek to justify normative ethical claims or consider the metaethical status of those normative claims. Importantly, in this project I have sought to follow the approach of Spinoza: "I have taken great care to understand human actions, and not to deride, deplore, or denounce them." (1958, 263).

So, if my project is not directly concerned with normative ethics or metaethics, what is it about? Put simply, this is a project in descriptive moral psychology. Talking purely descriptively about moral intuitions is difficult because the object of inquiry itself is concerned with moral categorisation. Take the example of the slavery. At some points in recorded human history, people have taken slavery to be permissible, and at other points in human history, people have taken slavery to be impermissible. Consider one person (at some point in human history) who finds themselves to have intuitively categorised slavery as morally impermissible, and another person (perhaps at another time in human history) who finds themselves to have intuitively categorised slavery as permissible. My project is to explain how both humans under consideration come to the positions they do based on the assumption that both humans are using the same biologically evolved cognitive systems to arrive at the two different positions. Now with what I hope is a clear distinction in place between normative ethics and metaethics, on the one hand, and descriptive moral psychology, on the other hand,

I will address the question: What am I referring to, when I say, 'moral intuition'? I take it to be the case that people regularly experience a particular psychological phenomenon of the following form. This phenomenon arises without deliberative reflection relevant to a set of circumstances that the person or others may be currently in, or may be imagining themselves or others in. One way of describing this phenomenon is that the person 'sees' the moral rightness or wrongness of the circumstances in question. Strictly speaking, the phenomenon is not a visual experience, so 'seeing' is not quite right, but it is not easy to describe this phenomenon. Furthermore, this phenomenon has a prescriptive force 'built in.' In other words, the phenomenon includes a 'feeling' of moral prescription. So, this phenomenon has features that are tolerably well (but not very well) characterised as 'seeing' and 'feeling' moral prescription in relation to morally relevant contexts.

So, I take it to be the case that most, if not all, people experience a particular class of psychological phenomena that are sufficiently similar to be grouped together into the class I will call 'moral intuition.' These phenomena occur in particular circumstances one finds oneself in (or perhaps imagines oneself in). They occur fast (one might say automatically), without psychological effort, and take the form of moral prescription. The way that one might describe intuitive moral categorisations to oneself, and others, varies. For example, one might say 'That is just wrong!' or 'I should do this!' (consider, for example, your own intuitions when you are faced with a choice between prioritising either justice or compassion). But importantly, propositions such as these are attempts to articulate the nature of the psychological phenomena in language. In a very important sense, these attempts are already one step removed from the phenomena itself.

Here are three characterisations of various subjects that help identify moral intuitions. The first is by Mill describing 'customary morality.'

[...] customary morality, that which education and opinion have consecrated, is the only one which presents itself to the mind with the feeling of being in itself obligatory; and when a person is asked to believe that this morality derives its obligation from some general principle around which custom has not thrown the same halo, the assertion is to him a paradox ... He says to himself, I feel that I am bound not to rob or murder, betray, or deceive; but why am I bound to promote the general happiness?

(1987, 28)

Mill notes that what he calls 'customary morality' is the only morality that has the feeling in and of itself of being obligatory. While I disagree with some of Mill's characterisation of this morality, and his name for it, I agree that this morality (involving what I call 'moral intuition') is the only one which 'presents itself to the mind with the feeling of being itself obligatory.'

The second characterisation relevant to what I call a 'moral intuition' is provided by Mackie. Mackie observes that "ordinary moral judgements include a claim to objectivity, an assumption that there are objective values [...] most people in making moral judgements implicitly claim, among other things, to be pointing to something objectively prescriptive, [...]." (1977, 35). He also observes that:

> An objective good would be sought by anyone who was acquainted with it, not because of any contingent fact that this person, or every person, is so constituted that he desires this end, but just because the end has to-be-pursuedness somehow built into it. Similarly, if there were objective principles of right and wrong, any wrong (possible) course of action would have not-to-be-doneness somehow built into it.
>
> (1977, 40)

Mackie identifies a 'to-be-pursuedness' or (in different circumstances) a 'not-to-be-doneness' in reference to potential courses of action. I take this to be an important insight, but I won't focus on Mackie's own project here (a project in metaethical 'error theory'). Rather, I want to focus on both 'to-be-pursuedness' and 'not-to-be-doneness' as psychological phenomena. In my eyes, Mackie's (1977, 40) characterisations that some "end has a to-be-pursuedness somehow built into it" and that "any wrong (possible) course of action would have a not-to-be-doneness somehow built into it" are very insightful. I take them to accurately characterise certain psychological phenomena. I assume that humans do experience 'to-be-pursuedness' and 'not-to-be doneness' in certain morally relevant contexts.

Finally, the third characterisation I will provide, one that will have a central place in this book, is offered by Rawls.

> Let us assume that each person beyond a certain age and possessed of the requisite intellectual capacity develops a sense of justice under normal social circumstances. We acquire a skill in judging things to be just and unjust, and in supporting these judgments by reasons. Moreover, we ordinarily have some desire to act

in accord with these pronouncements and expect a similar desire
on the part of others.

(Rawls 1973, 46)

Note that Rawls characterises the 'sense of justice' as a skill that, in
most people, is accompanied by a desire to act in accord with the pronouncements that the skill delivers.

I take it that these three writers have all identified the same psychological phenomena. They have called it different things, Mill calls it
'customary morality,' Mackie calls it 'ordinary moral judgement,' and
Rawls calls it a 'sense of justice' (and they all identify it for different
reasons). But, I hold that they are all identifying the same class of phenomena I call 'moral intuition.'

Importantly, I take it to be the case that the psychological phenomena
that I am describing is not an emotional reaction. An emotional reaction may be caused by a moral intuition, but it is distinct from it, even
though it may be very difficult to discriminate introspectively between
the moral intuition and any emotional reaction one might have to the
intuitive moral categorisation itself. The claim central to this book, and
the claim central to others applying the linguistic analogy (Huebner,
Dwyer, and Hauser 2009; Huebner 2015), is that whatever association
emotion does or does not have with moral judgement, it is not the source
of the judgement. I suggest that the emotional reaction in the context of
intuitive moral categorisation is a down-stream product (or by-product)
of the actual process producing the moral intuition itself. It is this process that is of interest to me. This is the process doing the intuitive judging. This process is the cause of moral intuition (understood as an output
of one or more cognitive systems) and precedes the emotional reaction.
By way of analogy, imagine that every time you saw the colour red you
got angry. I am interested in the process that made you see red, rather
than the fact that seeing red caused you to get angry. Emotion (or affect)
has a central place in much moral psychology research (Nichols 2008;
Greene 2015), but I, along with others (Huebner, Dwyer, and Hauser
2009), suggest the focus should be on what cognitive processes precede,
and possibly cause, the emotional responses. I hope that is enough to
demarcate in broad terms what I mean by moral intuition.

## Evolutionary analysis

I endorse what Samuels calls evolutionary analysis. This is "a strategy
for generating hypotheses about the structure of the human mind by
analysing the adaptive problems whose successful solution would have

contributed to reproductive success in the environment in which our evolutionary ancestors lived..." (2000, 24). Central to such analysis is what is called the 'environment of evolutionary adaptedness' (EEA). While some researchers use a temporally shallow definition of what they take to be the relevant EEA, that being the Pleistocene (Barrett, Dunbar, and Lycett 2002, 12), I use a temporally deep definition of the EEA. The human mind, as it exists now, is the result of a very long evolutionary history, and throughout that history, I assume that the evolutionary precursors to the human mind have consistently been subject to evolutionary pressures. Here, I am taking a very long view, starting with the first emergence of minds in our distant evolutionary ancestors. But to make this analysis more manageable, consider the evolutionary lineage of social mammals, which, evidence suggests, began at least 75 million years ago (Weaver et al. 2021).

Since before social mammals emerged in our evolutionary lineage, cognitive systems have been under selective pressure along many different dimensions. But again, to make this analysis more manageable, consider just three dimensions of evolutionary pressure, the selection of cognitive systems for prediction, social coordination, and communication. These have been, and continue to be, very important aspects of life for social mammals. The cognitive systems of social mammals have consistently been under selective pressure to (1) effectively predict events in their environment, (2) effectively coordinate social interactions, and (3) communicate effectively with one another. Specifically, I assume that these adaptive problems have exerted sufficiently strong selective pressure on the minds of our ancestors (via evolutionary processes) such as to sculpt the actual structure of human minds and the actual processes underway within those minds. And because these evolutionary pressures do not all act in the one direction, evolutionary analysis suggests these pressures would have produced a number of distinct structures and processes. Call these structures and processes that have a long causal-historical evolutionary history 'evolutionarily deep and distinct structures and processes.' The existence of these structures and processes in the mind is in significant tension with the assumption that the human mind is, at birth, a blank slate (Pinker 2003). So, this book assumes that the ways to think about the development of the mind endorsed within Evolutionary Psychology are the appropriate ways to understand the mind, rather than what advocates of Evolutionary Psychology identify as the Standard Social Science Model (Barkow, Cosmides, and Tooby 1992, 23).

## Evolutionarily deep and distinct structures and processes

I am assuming that distinct evolutionary pressures have sculpted human minds in distinct ways. And, these distinct pressures 'pushed' or 'pulled' the mind in very different directions. The concept of Design Space (Dennett 1996, 85) helps one to imagine this process of 'pushing' and 'pulling.' Imagine the various evolutionary challenges and opportunities faced by the mind represented, in the abstract, by different dimensions in an abstract multidimensional space. Evolution 'pushes' or 'pulls' along these dimensions, and this evolutionary pressure results in changes in the characteristics of the mind.[4]

Perhaps somewhat mysteriously (given the evolutionary origins of the mind that I am assuming in this book), when we introspect, we experience a reasonably unified conscious realm, which Dennett has called the 'Cartesian Theatre' (1991a, 17). But this experience only serves to obscure the fact (a fact assumed here) that the elements of conscience awareness are the result of many and varied evolutionary pressures. The evolutionary processes that led to conscious awareness were underway well before members of our lineage were conscious (or so I will assume). So, there is no reason to assume that this was a unified process. Indeed, taking evolutionary analysis seriously, we should assume that evolutionary pressures would in fact 'pull' and 'push' the mind in different directions. Thus, the unity of consciousness (such as it is) may be a recent phenomenon in evolutionary time.

One way to appreciate this fact is to consider the first personal experience of vision. As explained by McIlwain, humans are among the animals that:

> have two types of photoreceptors, one suited for low and the other for high light levels. Under dark-adapted conditions (scotopic vision), the highly sensitive rods permit the eye to see dim objects. When light levels are high (photopic vision), various adaptive mechanisms render the rods less sensitive than the cones, which then dominate the responses of the retina to light. Figuratively speaking, then, the human eye can switch between two retinas, one for low light levels and the other for high, and for this reason the human retina is said to be duplex. "Switching" may not be exactly the right word, because both the rod and cone systems can operate at the same time under some conditions.
>
> (McIlwain 1996, 92)

So, on the one hand, a particular set of evolutionary pressures, relevant to navigating in low light level conditions, have led to the evolution of rods, and on the other hand, a different set of evolutionary pressures, relevant to navigating in high light level conditions, have led to the evolution of cones. Notice that I used the word 'navigating' and not 'seeing' in the previous sentence. I take it that 'seeing' is connected to conscious awareness, but it is possible this journey through Design Space taken by the deep and distinct cognitive structures and processes that end with either rods or cones began before our ancestors were conscious. But now (again speaking figuratively), we 'see' with both our rods and cones. But introspectively, humans are not aware of the fact that they are 'seeing with rods' or 'seeing with cones.' Humans are just aware of the fact that they are 'seeing.'

I suggest that the same goes for many areas of human conscious awareness. Introspectively, we experience a reasonably unified conscious realm, but the parts of that seemingly unified whole have, I suggest, radically different causal–historical evolutionary origins. We should consider the deep evolutionary origins of the content and functioning of the mind when we attempt to understand the human capacity for prediction, social coordination, and communication. I further suggest that evolutionary pressures relating to prediction, social coordination, and communication have generated deep and distinct structures and processes in the mind. To reinforce this point, consider again the two parallel routes that lead to the experience of 'seeing.' There are two parallel sets of structures that lead ultimately to 'seeing.' Just because we have a reasonably unified experience of 'seeing,' we should not assume that 'seeing' is unified 'all the way down.' Similarly, I suggest that while all the thoughts we have about prediction, social coordination, and communication may present themselves in much the same way to conscious awareness, importantly, we should not assume that 'thinking' is unified 'all the way down.' I take Dennett's use of the idea of Pandemonium to be another version of this assumption. For example, he has suggested that language generation involves "opportunistic, parallel, evolutionary processes – almost all the way down" (Dennett 1991a, 242). Now, for the record, focusing on the three evolutionary pressures of prediction, social coordination, and communication is not intended to exhaust the set of evolutionary pressures. They simply serve to illustrate the idea I am presenting.

I take the suggestion, that there are deep and distinct structures and processes in the mind that have been shaped by evolutionary pressures, to be supported by work done by Spelke and Kinzler, who claim that humans have four core knowledge systems that represent "inanimate objects and their mechanical interactions, agents and their goal-directed actions, sets and their numerical relationships of ordering, addition and subtraction and places in the spatial layout and their geometric relationships" (Spelke and Kinzler 2007, 89). The object system identified by Spelke and Kinzler involves representing cohesion, continuity, and contact, while in contrast, the agent system is not based on spatial factors. The agent system representations do not need to involve cohesiveness, continuity, or direct physical contact. Rather, agent system representations involve actions that are goal-directed, efficient, contingent, and reciprocal.

I suggest that the object system will be central to the larger set of processes in the mind involved in the prediction of physical objects and that the agent system will be central to the larger set of processes in the mind involved in both social coordination and communication.

At the level of conscious awareness, introspectively, we may experience 'thinking about objects' and 'thinking about agents' in much the same way, and to such an extent that we assume that we are using the same set of cognitive systems to think about both. But, I am suggesting that in the very same way that the process of 'seeing with rods' and 'seeing with cones' involves distinct systems, namely, the rods and cones respectively, the process of 'thinking about objects' and 'thinking about agents' involves distinct systems, namely, the object core knowledge system and the agent core knowledge system. Similarly, I am suggesting that thoughts about prediction, thoughts about social coordination, and thoughts about communication may involve distinct systems in the mind. For example, thoughts about the prediction of physical objects presumably involve the object core knowledge system. The thoughts may or may not start there, but presumably the object core knowledge system will be somewhere within the network of systems and processes within the human body related to thoughts about the prediction of physical objects. And, thoughts about social coordination with agents presumably involve the agent core knowledge system. Again, the thoughts may or may not start there, but presumably, the agent core knowledge system will be somewhere within the network of systems and processes within the human body related to thoughts about the social coordination among agents. It is possible that both the human language faculty and the human moral faculty (understood as the systems and processes being discussed in this book) are two further core knowledge systems.

## Modularity and multi-level analysis of the mind

Another relevant way to think about the mind is in terms of modularity. Fodor (1983) suggests the existence of what he calls 'peripheral modules' in the mind. He identifies a number of features of peripheral modules, but two features of these modules are particularly relevant to the present discussion, namely, that the outputs of modules are "mandatory" and that the manipulations made inside modules are "relatively inaccessible to consciousness" (1983, 55). Fodor further elaborates on the relationship between these two features (using the human capacity to hear sentences in a natural language) as follows: "Not only must you hear an utterance of a sentence as such, but, to first approximation, you can hear it only that way" (1983, 55). And there appears to be something similar going on in the visual system in the case of the Müller-Lyer illusion (where two horizontal lines of equal length appear to be of unequal length due to the location of inwardly and outwardly facing pairs of chevrons at the ends of horizontal line), as illustrated in Figure 1.1.

Given the appropriate experiences (that may be culturally specific and involve experiencing rectangular shapes during psychological development), some humans cannot but see the two horizontal lines as having different lengths (Segall, Campbell, and Herskovit 1966). This illusion suggests that the visual system is also to some extent subject to modular architecture because it is not possible not to see the lines as having different lengths even after one knows them to be of equal length.

Since Fodor proposed the existence of peripheral modules, others have further developed the idea of modularity in a number of ways (e.g. Samuels, Stich, and Tremoulet 1999, 91; Carruthers 2006). Here is how Cosmides and Tooby characterise the so-called Massive Modularity Hypothesis:[5]

> [O]ur cognitive architecture resembles a confederation of hundreds or thousands of functionally dedicated computers (often called modules) designed to solve adaptive problems endemic to our hunter-gatherer ancestors. Each of these devices has its own agenda and imposes its own exotic organization on different fragments of the world. There are specialized systems for grammar induction, for face recognition, for dead reckoning, for construing objects and for recognizing emotions from the face. There are mechanisms to detect animacy, eye direction, and cheating. There is a "theory of mind" module…. a variety of social inference modules…. and a multitude of other elegant machines.
>
> (1995, xiv)

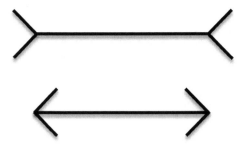

*Figure 1.1* The Müller-Lyer Illusion.

What Spelke and Kinzler are saying about core knowledge systems, what Fodor is saying about peripheral modules, and what others are saying about massive modularity are importantly related. Both core knowledge systems and modules (either peripheral or otherwise) are parts of the deep and distinct structures and processes in the mind. The reason we think in terms of physical objects and their mechanical interactions, or we think in terms of agents and their goal directed actions, is because of the existence in our mind of the structures and processes that generate these thoughts – structures and processes that are shaped by evolution. In the very same way, the reason we hear sounds as words or sentences is because of the existence in our mind of the structures and processes that generate those thoughts – structures and processes that are also shaped by evolution. In this book, I develop the suggestion that the reason we perceive certain contexts in moral terms is because of the existence in our mind of structures and processes that generate those thoughts as moral intuitions. The structures and processes that lead to humans seeing the world in moral terms are also shaped by evolution.

Finally, in this section, I will say a few words about multi-level theories of cognition. The idea that the mind is not one unified realm goes back a reasonably long way. Plato (1993) conceived of the soul (the soul being close enough to the mind for our current purposes) as tripartite, being comprised of reason, spirit, and appetite.[6] But more recently, an academic research programme is developing exploring the possibility of a multi-system (or multi-process) mind that generally goes by the name of dual-system or dual-process theory (Reber 1993; Evans and Over 1996; Sloman 1996; Stanovich and West 2000; Evans and Frankish

2009).[7] Now, it may well transpire that thinking in terms of two systems is not the most accurate way to characterise the structure of the mind, but it will do for present purposes.[8] The central suggestion here is that the human mind is composed of (at least) two systems, System 1 and System 2. The specific detail of the two systems is not centrally important to my claims in this book. But, I assume that there are (at least) two systems, that may have all, or some, of the following characteristics (Evans and Frankish 2009, 15).

System 1: evolutionarily old, unconscious, preconscious, shared with animals, implicit knowledge, automatic, fast, parallel, high capacity, intuitive, contextualized, pragmatic, associative, independent of general intelligence.

System 2: evolutionarily recent, conscious, uniquely/distinctively human, explicit knowledge, controlled, slow, sequential, low capacity, reflective, abstract, logical, rule-based, linked to general intelligence.[9]

The cognitive systems and/or processes that I claim generate moral intuitions may not have all the characteristics listed above. But, I assume this general division between System 1 and System 2 is directly relevant to understanding the nature of moral intuitions, and furthermore, I assume that moral intuitions are produced by systems that feature a number of the characteristics of System 1.

Here is how Stanovich and West (2000, 659) characterise the distinction between the two systems: System 1 (intuition) is fast, automatic, undemanding of cognitive capacity, and acquired by biology, exposure, and personal experience; and System 2 (reasoning) is slow, controlled, demanding of cognitive capacity, and acquired by cultural and formal instruction. And, Kahneman in his Nobel Prize Lecture also gives a useful insight into the distinction between the two by describing System 1 as producing intuitive judgements that "occupy a position – perhaps corresponding to evolutionary history – between the automatic operations of perception and the deliberate operations of reasoning" (2002, 450). This, to my mind, is very similar to the insight offered by Rawls (1973, 46): "Let us assume that each person beyond a certain age and possessed of the requisite intellectual capacity develops a sense of justice under normal social circumstances." I suggest that the production and consumption of moral intuitions is to be understood as one or more System 1 process, and Rawls' sense of justice is an output of System 1.

## Applying the 'tri-level' hypothesis from within cognitive science

This book draws on cognitive science. But, cognitive science is a broad area of inquiry. I will use a very specific dimension of cognitive science in my analysis of moral intuition, and that is what has become known as the 'tri-level hypothesis.' This hypothesis relates to attempts to understand information-processing systems in general (be those information-processing systems within biological organisms or otherwise). I take the systems that generate moral intuitions to be a form of information-processing system, so this hypothesis is relevant to our understanding of these systems. There are a number of ways to understand the 'tri-level hypothesis.' Pylyshyn (1999, 7) identifies three levels at which generalisations can be made about how intelligent systems are organised: (1) the knowledge or semantic level; (2) the symbolic or syntactic level; and (3) the biological or physical level. And before him, Marr (1982, 24) characterised three levels – "at which an information-processing device must be understood before one can be said to have understood it completely" – with reference to three sets of questions:

> The Computational Theory What is the goal of the computation, why is it appropriate, and what is the logic of the strategy by which it can be carried out?
>
> Representation and algorithm: How can this computational theory be implemented? In particular, what is the representation for the input and output, and what is the algorithm for the transformation?
>
> Hardware implementation: How can the representation and algorithm be realised physically?
>
> (1982, 24)

What I have to say in this book concerns the first two levels identified by Marr and Pylyshyn. What Marr calls the computational level and the representational/algorithmic level, and what Pylyshyn calls the semantic level and the syntactic level.[10]

So, how does the tri-level hypothesis relate to moral intuitions? Well, I can answer this question in very broad terms here by providing some answers to some of Marr's questions. To answer Marr's question: what is the goal of the computation? The goal of the set of computations in which moral intuitions play a role is social coordination. And, I say 'social coordination' rather than 'social cooperation' very deliberately because I take social coordination to be a wider category than social cooperation. Some forms of social coordination, such as slavery, may not necessarily be understood as 'social cooperation,' but they are forms of 'social coordination.' Throughout our evolutionary history, effective coordination with social groups was essential for survival, and so it should be no surprise that evolutionary pressures have resulted in the generation of a system of moral intuitions that would further social coordination within groups.[11]

To answer Marr's question: What is the representation for the input and output, and what is the algorithm for the transformation? The inputs to one of the relevant transformations are what I call morally relevant elements within morally relevant contexts,[12] and the outputs are moral intuitions that take the form of prescriptions such as the 'to-be-pursuedness' or 'not-to-be-doneness' so perceptively identified by Mackie, or the 'obligatory' customary morality of Mill (or more generally, the intuitive moral categorisations 'impermissible' or 'obligatory,' etc.).

When considering Pylyshyn's distinction between semantics and syntax, it is important to note that I am using the concept of 'categorisation' (within my concept of 'moral intuition') in a particular way that is importantly similar to the idea of meaning.

At the level of semantics, moral intuitions have 'meanings.' Think of the meanings as the categories themselves. And those meanings are very simple, the meanings include prescriptions such as 'impermissible' or 'obligatory' when understood as a moral prescription. And at the level of syntax, the concept of grammatical and ungrammatical arrangements of elements is central. Morally grammatical arrangements of elements have moral meaning at the semantic level (they might mean 'obligatory' or 'impermissible'). But, morally ungrammatical strings of elements have no moral meaning at all. They simply don't register as morally relevant. Or perhaps, they might be taken to be 'permissible' by default in the sense of being neither 'impermissible' nor 'obligatory.' The analogy between moral intuition and natural language is central to this book and for good reason. Natural languages have commonalities but also differences across human groups, just as the sets of moral intuitions shared within human groups have commonalities and differences across human groups.

Before I move on, a word needs to be said about the third level of the 'tri-level hypothesis,' the level of physical implementation. I won't say much about this level, simply because I don't have much to say about it. There are significant challenges facing those who wish to give an account of how the computations and algorithms discussed at levels three and two are instantiated at level one in the case of moral intuitions. For example, the question of how to relate the computational activity discussed in cognitive science to the neural activity discussed in neuroscience is yet to be answered. So, I will leave that question for others.

## Drawing the linguistic analogy in moral psychology

There is disagreement among psycholinguists about whether the human capacity for language is due to general cognitive capacities or specific cognitive capacities that evolved independently as a result of specific evolutionary pressures (Harley 2014, 26). In this book, I assume that the human capacity for language is the result of specific cognitive capacities that evolved independently due to specific evolutionary pressures associated with communication. Recall Dennett's concept of an abstract Design Space. One or more dimensions of that space are directly relevant to the abstract capacity to communicate, and evolution 'pushed' or 'pulled' along those dimensions, and this resulted in the evolution of a lineage of organisms that have features that allow them to communicate. Some of those features are anatomical features outside the mind (e.g. features of the human larynx), but other of those features are structures and processes within the mind. There are several ways to think about the features of the mind that allow for the human capacity for language. But one way to think is terms of a language faculty and I will think in these terms here. Hauser, Chomsky, and Fitch (2002, 1569) make a distinction between the language faculty in a broad and narrow sense and suggest that the broad sense "includes a sensory-motor system, a conceptual-intentional system, and the computational mechanisms for recursion, providing the capacity to generate an infinite range of expressions from a finite set of elements."[13] They further suggest that the language faculty in a narrow sense only includes the capacity for recursion. Whether or not Hauser et al. have all the details correct is not centrally important here. What is centrally important is that they distinguish a broad sense of the language faculty and a narrow sense of the language faculty. I will be using a similar approach when exploring the moral faculty (where this refers to the cognitive systems and processes that generate moral intuitions).

Just as is the case with psycholinguists, there is disagreement among philosophers and psychologists about whether the human capacity for morality is due to general cognitive capacities or specific cognitive capacities (that evolved independently due to specific evolutionary pressures). In this book, I will be assuming that there exists a moral faculty in the same way that Hauser et al assume there exists a language faculty. And to simply adapt the distinction used by Hauser et al., I will make a distinction between the moral faculty in a broad and narrow sense and suggest that the broad sense of the moral faculty includes a sensory-motor system, a conceptual-intentional system, and the computational mechanisms providing the capacity to interpret and generate an infinite range of intuitive moral categorisations within morally salient contexts. For example, it includes Spelke and Kinzler's agent core knowledge system. I further suggest, again adapting the distinction used by Hauser et al., that the moral faculty in a narrow sense only includes the computational systems and processes providing the capacity to interpret and generate an infinite range of intuitive moral categorisations within morally relevant contexts. These computational systems and processes are the ones identified in the process of answering the questions posed by Marr at his computational level ("What is the goal of the computation, why is it appropriate, and what is the logic of the strategy by which it can be carried out?") and representational/algorithmic level ("How can this computational theory be implemented? In particular, what is the representation for the input and output, and what is the algorithm for the transformation?") (Marr 1982).

And, I assume that the computational systems and processes that constitute the moral faculty (understood in the narrow sense) have arisen due to evolutionary pressure. Identifying the detail of the structure of the computations and identifying the computational systems and processes that instantiate those computations is the subject matter of the Moralistics and Psychomoralistics research programmes. But, at this early stage in the emergence of these research programmes, I don't think it is useful to make commitments relating to the detailed nature of the 'moral faculty' understood in the narrow sense. Humans have auditory systems that produce the experience of hearing sounds, and somewhere within or downstream of that auditory system is a system that allows (and, indeed, demands) that certain sounds to be heard as words (Fodor 1983, 55). I suggest that something equivalent is going on with reference to the interpretation of certain situations as morally meaningful. I think it is wrong to assume that all the computational complexity that presumably exists within the language faculty is needed for the functioning of a moral faculty. But, the simple idea of a faculty that intuitively recognises a state of affairs as (1) morally meaningful, and furthermore as (2) morally obligatory or morally impermissible, is essentially right. And, by analogy, it is equivalent to the intuitive ability to (1) recognise certain sounds as words and sentences, (2) determine whether a sentence in one's natural language is grammatical (equivalent to being morally meaningful), and (3) attribute particular meaning to that sentence (equivalent to the moral meanings morally obligatory, or morally impermissible, etc.).

I assume that there is a moral faculty. Of course, there are those who disagree. Johnson (2012) argues that there is no moral faculty, and he claims that advocates of a moral faculty are motivated by the idea that the existence of a moral faculty supports the idea that there are universal moral norms. But, it is important to note that the existence of a language faculty does not lead to the existence of only one natural language. Rather, the language faculty (assuming one exists) allows for the production of many languages. Analogously, I assume that if a moral faculty exists, it will also allow for the production of many intuitive moralities (where intuitive morality is understood as a set of intuitive moral categorisations). Indeed, this is an assumption shared by advocates of the Linguistic Analogy in Moral Psychology and Moral Foundations Theory (Dwyer, Huebner, and Hauser 2010; Graham et al. 2013). One of the interesting empirical questions in a newly unified cognitive science of moral intuition (an empirical question already being considered within Moral Foundations Theory and the Linguistics Analogy in Moral Psychology) will be this: what are the constraints that exist such that only certain moralities will be produced by the moral faculty? And importantly, I think that the empirical methods of anthropology, psychology, cognitive science, and neuroscience are the methods to use when investigating the production and consumption of moral intuitions as produced by a moral faculty (and consumed by other parts of the mind). This is broadly equivalent to the approach and assumptions of those who study the language faculty.

In the fullness of time, it may transpire that there is no moral faculty and if so, then whatever scientific research was directed towards the study of that faculty was ultimately fruitless. This is simply the nature of scientific research. But that is no reason not to pursue scientific research. I expect that the scientific research will uncover a moral faculty and that research will be able to offer insight into a number of what Brown calls human universals such as distinguishing right and wrong, redress of wrongs, moral sentiments, and the limited effective range of moral sentiments (Brown 1991).

## Moralistics and Psychomoralistics is the study of 'moral intuitions'

The subject matter of Moralistics and Psychomoralistics is how cognitive systems and processes generate what the person in the street would pre-theoretically label as a moral intuition. This assumes that there is a class of cognitive output that is well defined enough to call moral intuition, in the same way that there is a class of cognitive output that is well defined enough to call judgements about the grammaticality of sentences in natural language.

Another way to put this is to say that just as we can interpret certain sounds we hear as words, we can interpret certain situations as morally meaningful. So just as when you hear a person talking in your native language, you are aware of that linguistic context, you may experience some situation in terms of moral meaning, and, thus, you are aware of that moral context. An example of moving from a non-moral context to a moral context helps make the point. Imagine you are shooting at a target in a designated archery range with no humans (or other sentient animals if one's intuitive moral obligations extend to sentient animals) in the area of the target so that there is no chance that you could accidently shoot a human (or other sentient animal) with your arrow. I suggest you are not in a morally meaningful context, and I further suggest you would not be aware of any moral intuitions. But notice the change if a person (or sentient animal) appears close to your target. Suddenly, I suggest, you are in a morally meaningful context. Let's say for the sake of argument that you feel it would be morally impermissible to continue to shoot at the target while the person (or sentient animal) is near the target because it is a possibility that you might harm them. So, I suggest you would suddenly become aware of a moral intuition that it would be impermissible to continue shooting arrows.

So, what needs to be the case for this project to have an object of study? There needs to be class of mental output that (1) is not largely random, (2) is not attributable to some other mental process, e.g. emotion, and (3) is suitably analysable in terms of the 'tri-level hypothesis.' If it turns out that what I am calling moral intuition is just an output of an emotional system, then I should simply concede that this is the study of emotion not the study of moral intuition. But I contend that it is not the case. I am not simply mislabelling the outputs of emotional systems as moral intuitions. I think that there is a subject matter for this research. So, I am interested in the nature and origin of these moral intuitions.

Is there a clearly defined class of moral intuitions? I suggest that there is.[14] So what is used to define the boundary of this class of intuitions? Let us assume, for argument's sake, that there is a language faculty, so we can use that faculty to define the boundary of relevant sounds. Spoken language is made up of the sounds that are interpreted as language by the language faculty. So, by analogy, moral intuitions relate to contexts that are interpreted as morally meaningful by the moral faculty. If we assume there is a moral faculty, then moral intuitions are that which is produced and consumed by the moral faculty. If there is a moral faculty, then the task is to explore the sorts of intuitions that that faculty produces and how that faculty produces them. This is directly analogous to the thought that there is a language faculty that allows us to produce grammatical sentences in our native language. The simple fact that we can both understand and produce grammatical sentences is remarkable. I think it is equally remarkable that we are able to intuitively categorise morally permissible and morally impermissible behaviours in morally meaningful social contexts. Again, I stress, this project is not centrally concerned with which particular behaviours are taken to be morally obligatory, or morally impermissible in any particular context (that, I assume, will vary across social groups). What I am interested in, and what I think is remarkable, is that we are able to think in moral terms at all. So, the interesting question, equivalent to the question 'How are we even able to use language?' is 'How are we even able to use morality?'

One answer to the question 'How are we even able to use morality?' is that moral intuitions are part of the inheritance we received from evolution. Indeed, I suspect the only reason we find ourselves motivated to deliberate about moral questions, using System 2, is because we have the example of moral intuitions, produced by System 1. I further suspect that if we did not have the moral intuitions, that are the outputs of System 1, it would never occur, to System 2, to deliberate about moral questions. In other words, without the existence of moral intuitions produced by System 1, the very concept morality (as opposed to other concepts like self-interested cooperation) would not exist and would not be deliberated upon at all. This is exactly equivalent to the perception of colour. If humans did not experience the world visually in terms of colours (among other aspects of visual experience), then humans would not spend any time deliberating about the nature of colour. One obvious and significant difference between the perception of colour and the experience of moral intuitions is the experiences of moral intuition have, in Mackie's insightful phrases, a 'to-be-pursuedness' or a 'not to be doneness' essentially built in (1977, 40), whereas the perception of colour does not. But, I suggest, there is nothing mysterious here. Intuitively judging 'the good' and seeing 'colour' are similar processes and neither 'the good (understood intuitively)' nor 'colour' exist independently of interpretation.[15] Of course, one can deliberate upon what to do, and one can come to a decision about what to do, and this can be motivated by many different motivations, for example, self-interest, fear of punishment, or political expediency. But, I suggest that none of these come with the built in 'to be pursuedness' or 'not to be doneness,' that is the essential hallmark of moral intuition as I understand it here.

## One sense of normativity that is relevant to this project

This project is not centrally concerned with normative ethics nor metaethics. But there are ways to understand a normative question within descriptive moral psychology as well, so I want to note this sense of the normative.

Assume that a moral faculty is generating moral intuitions as outputs. The purpose of the cognitive science of moral intuition is to understand the systems and processes that generate moral intuitions. The word 'understand' has a normative dimension. There are some accounts that provide understanding and others that don't. This sense of normativity – providing understanding – is relevant to the cognitive science of moral intuition.[16]

The scientific project advanced in this book is to understand how moral intuitions are produced, and so we need to know if the systems producing them are working as they 'should' – in the same way that we can ask is the visual system, or the cardiopulmonary system, working as it 'should.'

The visual system is working as it should when it functions as it evolved to function. But when we ask the same question of the moral faculty (Is the moral faculty working as it should?), there is a confound between two senses of 'should.' 'Is it working in a consistent manner in the context of its evolution, development, and implementation?', is one way to ask the question. And this is a relevant question at the level of the description of the moral faculty. But, there is another level at which one can ask the question and that is at the philosophical level. This question is not a question about the implementation of a certain process or whether the system is working 'normally,' but whether the system is generating (according to some people) the 'morally correct' output. This philosophical question is not the topic of this book. It is, of course, not surprising that confusion is possible in this context because, as mentioned above, unlike the outputs of the visual system, the outputs of the moral faculty are, from a first personal perspective, themselves normative in nature. But, it is important to distinguish the two senses in which the concept of normative can be applied in this context. Some paired questions will make this distinction clear. Consider the following questions:

1A Is the visual system functioning as it evolved to function?
1B Should the visual system be functioning this way?
2A Is the cardiopulmonary system functioning as it evolved to function?
2B Should the cardiopulmonary system be functioning this way?

The first question in each of the above pairs seems like a reasonable question, but if the answer to the first question was 'yes,' then the second question in each pair would seem odd. But now, consider the equivalent pair of questions in the context of morality.

3A Is the moral faculty functioning as it evolved to function?
3B Should the moral faculty be functioning this way?

The first question in every pair of questions above is a scientific question (or so I assume). And, the scientific question about the moral faculty is the topic of this book. The second question in the pair of moral questions does not seem odd in the way that the second questions in each of the first two pairs seem odd because it leads off into a radically different (philosophical) debate. That debate, interesting though it is, is not the topic of this book.

There is a final sense of normativity that needs to be noted. The question of whether a sentence in natural language is taken to be grammatical is settled by competent users of that language.[17] In one sense, this is a normative question, in that competent uses of that language will characterise the sentence as either grammatically correct or not. But in another sense, this is a descriptive question, in that an observer wishing to know the answer simply needs to observe the answers provided by competent users of that language.[18] If competent users say it is grammatically correct, then it is grammatically correct.[19] In the same way, if competent users of an intuitive moral language deem a potential act in a moral context to be intuitively morally impermissible, then it is intuitively morally impermissible. If an observer does not share the moral intuition, the observer is simply using a different intuitive moral language.[20]

**Summary of chapter**

In this chapter, I have presented the theoretical framework in which this project is located. Put very simply this project is located within evolutionary psychology and assumes that the mind includes systems and processes shaped by evolution that facilitate social coordination within groups of humans by intuitively categorising actual or possible states of affairs within morally relevant contexts as morally impermissible or obligatory, etc.

**Notes**

1 Here I refer to moral codes that were stable enough to facilitate human social coordination that persisted long enough to be recorded, for example, the Code of Hammurabi (1750 BC).

2 Impermissible and obligatory are two examples, further research may identify more, such as 'good' understood as intuitively morally good, or 'bad' understood as intuitively morally bad.

3 Evolutionary Psychology means different things to different people. For an overview see (Laland and Brown 2011).

4 Here I am simply ignoring the fact that there is complex string of causal relationships that lead to selective pressure on 'the mind'.

5 While I consider modules to play a role, in some way, in the account I present in this book, it should be noted that the Massive Modularity Hypothesis is not without its critics (Zerilli 2021).

6 Perhaps the best place to locate the moral intuitions I discuss here are within what Plato calls spirit. And there are similarities here with the tripartite conceptualisation of attitude structure, constituted by cognition, affective evaluation, and behavioural disposition (DeLamater and Collett 2018, 249).

7 For an overview of this research programme see Evans and Frankish (2009)

8 It is interesting to note that some are now considering (returning to?) a tripartite division (Stanovich 2009).

9 The inclusion of the relationship to general intelligence raises a number of issues that are beyond the scope of this paper, but see (Stanovich and West 2008) for a relevant discussion.

10 Others applying the linguistic analogy have also identified the centrality of computation in their analysis (Dwyer, Huebner, and Hauser 2010).

11 I am aware of the ongoing discussion about 'group selection' in biology, but I set this discussion aside in this book. For a review see (Leigh Jr 2010).

12 Presumably there is another process before this that transforms neutral elements within contexts into moral relevant elements within morally relevant contexts, but I set this aside in this description.

13 One of the papers that this paper itself references (titled 'Rule learning by cotton-top tamarins' published in 2002 by the journal Cognition) has now been retracted, but I do not consider this retraction to undermine the

reasonableness of the distinction made in this paper between the existence of a broad language faculty and a narrow language faculty that I draw upon in this book.

14 There is a parallel here with Dennett's concept of 'real patterns' but space limitations preclude an analysis (1991b).

15 I explore these themes in Wood (2020).

16 I am using the phrase 'providing understanding' here because I want my account to be relevant to both scientific realists and anti-realists.

17 When those users' performance is mapping onto their competence.

18 When those answers are provided while the user's performance corresponds to their competence.

19 And the same normative/descriptive distinction can be applied to the question of whether or not a user of a language is a competent user or not.

20 In this book I set aside a full discussion of so-called "I-grammar" (Roedder and Harman 2010, 276).

## References

Barkow, Jerome, Leda Cosmides, and John Tooby. 1992. *The Adapted Mind: Evolutionary Psychology and the Generation of Culture*. New York: Oxford University Press.

Barrett, Louise, Robin Dunbar, and John Lycett. 2002. *Human Evolutionary Psychology*. Princeton, NJ: Princeton University Press.

Brown, Donald E. 1991. *Human Universals*. Boston, MA: McGraw Hill.

Carruthers, Peter. 2006. *The Architecture of the Mind*. Oxford: Oxford University Press.

Cosmides, Leda, and John Tooby. 1992. "Cognitive Adaptations for Social Exchange." In *The Adapted Mind: Evolutionary Psychology and the Generation of Culture*, edited by Jerome Barkow, Leda Cosmides and John Tooby, 163–228. New York: Oxford University Press.

Cosmides, Leda, and John Tooby. 1995. *Foreword. In S. Baron-Cohen's Mindblindness: An Essay on Autism and Theory of Mind*. Cambridge, MA: MIT Press.

Cosmides, Leda, and John Tooby. 2008. "Can a General Deontic Logic Capture the Facts of Human Moral Reasoning? How the Mind Interprets Social Exchange Rules and Detects Cheaters." In *Moral Psychology Volume 1: The Evolution of Morality: Adaptations and Innateness*, edited by Walter Sinnott-Armstrong, 53–119. Cambridge, MA: MIT Press.

Cosmides, Leda, and John Tooby. 2015. "Adaptations for Reasoning About Social Exchange." In *The Handbook of Evolutionary Psychology*, edited by David M. Buss, 625–668. Hoboken, NJ: John Wiley & Sons.

Cosmides, Leda, John Tooby, and Jerome Barkow. 1992. "Introduction: Evolutionary Psychology and Conceptual Intergration." In *The Adapted Mind: Evolutionary Psychology and the Generation of Culture*, edited by Jerome Barkow, Leda Cosmides and John Tooby, 3–15. Oxford: Oxford University Press.

DeLamater, John, and Jessica Collett. 2018. *Social Psychology*. New York: Routledge.

Dennett, Daniel. 1991a. *Consciousness Explained*. London: Penguin.

Dennett, Daniel. 1991b. "Real Patterns." *The Journal of Philosophy* 88 (1):27–51.

Dennett, Daniel. 1996. *Darwin's Dangerous Idea: Evolution and the Meaning of Life*. London: Penguin Books.

Dwyer, Susan. 2007. "How Good is the Linguistic Analogy?" In *The Innate Mind: Volume 2: Culture and Cognition*, edited by Peter Carruthers, Stephen Laurence and Stephen Stich, 237–256. Oxford: Oxford University Press.

Dwyer, Susan, Bryce Huebner, and Marc D. Hauser. 2010. "The Linguistic Analogy: Motivations, Results, and Speculations." *Topics in Cognitive Science* 2:486–510.

Evans, Jonathan St. B. T., and Keith Frankish. 2009. *In Two Minds: Dual Processes and Beyond*. Oxford: Oxford University Press.

Evans, Jonathan St. B. T., and David E. Over. 1996. *Rationality and Reasoning*. Hove, UK: Psychology Press.

Fodor, Jerry. 1983. *The Modularity of Mind*. Cambridge: MIT.

Govier, Trudy, and Lowell Ayers. 2012. "Logic and Parables: Do These Naratives Provide Arguments?" *Informal Logic* 32 (2):161–189.

Graham, Jesse, Jonathan Haidt, Sena Koleva, Matt Motyl, Ravi Iyer, Sean Wojcik, and Peter Ditto. 2013. "Moral Foundations Theory: The Pragmatic Validity of Moral Pluralism." *Advances in Experimental Social Psychology* 47, 55–130.

Graham, Jesse, Jonathan Haidt, Matt Motyl, Peter Meindl, Carol Iskiwitch, and Marlon Mooijman. 2018. "Moral Foundations Theory: On the Advantages of Moral Pluralism over Moral Monism." In *Atlas of Moral Psychology*, edited by Kurt Gray and Jesse Graham, 211–222. New York: The Guilford Press.

Greene, Joshua D. 2015. *Moral Tribes: Emotion, Reason, and the Gap between Us and Them*. London: Atlantic Books.

Haidt, Jonathan, and Craig Joseph. 2007. "The Moral Mind: How Five Sets of Innate Intuitions Guide Development of Many Culture-Specific Virtues, and Perhaps Even Modules." In *The Innate Mind: Volume 3 Foundations and the Future*, edited by Peter Carruthers, Stephen Laurence and Stephen Stich, 367–392. Oxford: Oxford University Press.

Hammurabi. 1750 BC. "The Code of Hammurabi." Translated by L. W. King. In *The Avalon Project: Documents in Law, History and Diplomacy*. Yale Law School. https://avalon.law.yale.edu/ancient/hamframe.asp

Harley, Trevor. 2014. *The Psychology of Language: From Data to Theory*. New York: Psychology Press.

Hauser, Marc D., Noam Chomsky, and W. Tecumseh Fitch. 2002. "The Faculty of Language: What Is It, Who Has It, and How Did It Evolve?" *Science* 298 (5598), 1569–1579.

Huebner, Bryce. 2015. "Do Emotions Play a Constituitve Role in Moral Cognition?" *Topoi* 34 (2), 427–440.

Huebner, Bryce, Susan Dwyer, and Marc D. Hauser. 2009. "The Role of Emotion in Moral Psychology." *Trends in Cognitive Science* 13 (1), 1–6.

Johnson, Mark. 2012. "There Is No Moral Faculty." *Philosophical Psychology* 25 (3): 409–432.

Kahneman, Daniel. 2002. *Nobel Prize Lecture - Maps of Bounded Rationality: A Perspective on Intuitive Judgment and Choice.* Sweden: The Nobel Foundation, https://www.nobelprize.org/uploads/2018/06/kahnemann-lecture.pdf.

Laland, Kevin N., and Gillian R. Brown. 2011. *Sense and Nonsense.* 2nd ed. Oxford: Oxford University Press.

Leigh Jr, E. G. 2010. "The Group Selection Controversy." *Journal of Evolutionary Biology* 23:6–19.

Mackie, J. L. 1977. *Ethics: Inventing Right and Wrong.* London: Penguin.

Marr, David. 1982. *Vision : A Computational Investigation into the Human Representation and Processing of Visual Information.* San Francisco, CA: W. H. Freeman.

McIlwain, James T. 1996. *An Introduction to the Biology of Vision.* Cambridge: Cambridge University Press.

Mikhail, John. 2007. "Universal Moral Grammar: Theory, Evidence, and the Future." *Trends in Cognitive Science* 11 (4):143–152.

Mikhail, John. 2011. *Elements of Moral Cognition: Rawl's Linguistic Analogy and the Cognitive Science of Moral and Legal Judgment.* Cambridge: Cambridge University Press.

Mill, John, Stuart. 1991. *On Liberty and Other Essays.* Oxford: Oxford University Press. Original edition, 1859.

Nichols, Shaun. 2008. "Sentimentalism Naturalized." In *Moral Psychology Volume 2 The Cognitive Science of Morality: Intuition and Diversity*, edited by Walter Sinnott-Armstrong, 255–274. Cambridge: MIT Press.

Pinker, Steven. 2003. *The Blank Slate: The Modern Denial of Human Nature.* New York: Penguin Books.

Plato. 1993. *Republic.* Oxford: Oxford University Press.

Pylyshyn, Zenon. 1999. "What's in Your Mind?" In *What is Cognitive Science?*, edited by Ernest Lepore and Zenon Pylyshyn, 1–25. Oxford: Blackwell.

Rawls, John. 1973. *A Theory of Justice.* Oxford: Oxford University Press.

Reber, Arthur. 1993. *Implicit Learning and Tacit Knowledge: An Essay on the Cognitive Unconscious.* Oxford: Oxford University Press.

Roedder, Erica, and Gilbert H. Harman. 2010. "Linguistics and Moral Theory." In *The Moral Psychology Handbook*, edited by John Doris, 273–296. Oxford: Oxford University Press.

Samuels, Richard. 2000. "Massively Modular Minds: Evolutionary Psychology and Cognitive Architecture." In *Evolution and the Human Mind: Modularity, Language and Meta-Cognition*, edited by Peter Carruthers and Andrew Chamberlain, 13–46. Cambridge: Cambridge University Press.

Samuels, Richard, Stephen Stich, and Patrice Tremoulet. 1999. "Rethinking Rationality: From Bleak Implications to Darwinian Modules." In *What is Cognitive Science?*, edited by Ernest Lepore and Zenon Pylyshyn, 74–120. Oxford: Blackwell.

Saunders, Leland F. 2009. "Reason and Intuition in the Moral Life: A Dual-Process Account of Moral Justification." In *In Two Minds: Dual Processes and Beyond*, edited by Jonathan St. B. T. Evans and Keith Frankish, 335–354. Oxford: Oxford University Press.

Segall, Marshall H., T. Donald Campbell, and Melville J. Herskovit. 1966. *The Influence of Culture on Visual Perception*. Indianapolis, IN: Bobbs-Merrill.

Sloman, Steven. 1996. "The Emprical Case for Two Systems of Reasoning." *Psychological Bulletin* 119 (1):3–22.

Spelke, Elizabeth, and Katherine Kinzler. 2007. "Core Knowledge." *Developmental Science* 10 (1):89–96.

Spinoza, Baruch. 1958. *The Political Works*. Translated by A. G. Wernham. Oxford: Oxford University Press.

Sripada, Chandra Sekhar, and Stephen Stich. 2007. "A Framework for the Psychology of Norms." In *The Innate Mind: Volume 2: Culture and Cognition*, edited by Peter Carruthers, Stephen Laurence and Stephen Stich, 280–301, Oxford: Oxford University Press.

Stanovich, Keith E. 2009. "Distinguishing the Reflective, Algorithmic, and Autonomous Minds: Is It Time for a Tri-Process Theory?" In *In Two Minds: Dual Processes and Beyond*, edited by Jonathan St. B. T. Evans and Keith Frankish, 55–88. Oxford: Oxford University Press.

Stanovich, Keith E., and R. F. West. 2008. "On the Relative Independence of Thinking Biases and Cognitive Ability." *Journal of Personality and Social Psychology* 94 (4):672–695.

Stanovich, W., and R. F. West. 2000. "Individual Difference in Reasoning: Implications for the Rationality Debate?" *Behavioural and Brain Sciences* 23:645–726.

Weaver, Lucas N., David J. Varricchio, Eric J. Sargis, Meng Chen, William J. Freimuth, and Gregory P. Wilson Mantilla. 2021. "Early Mammalian Social Behaviour Revealed in Multituberculates from a Dinosaur Nesting Site." *Nature: Ecology & Evolution* 5:32–37.

Wood, Graham. 2020. "On the Perceived Objectivity of Some Moral Beliefs." *Philosophical Psychology* 33 (1):23–41.

Zerilli, John. 2021. *The Adaptable Mind: What Neuroplasticity and Neural Reuse Tell Us about Language and Cognition*. New York: Oxford University Press.

# 2 Unifying cognitive science of moral intuition

## Sketching the elephant

This chapter describes how a number of established research programmes in moral psychology can be combined to create a unified cognitive science of moral intuition. A re-framed Linguistic Analogy in Moral Psychology (Rawls 1973; Dwyer, Huebner, and Hauser 2010) will be used to unify Moral Foundations Theory (Haidt and Joseph 2004; Graham et al. 2013) and Cognitive Adaptations for Social Exchange (Cosmides and Tooby 1992, 2015), into what I call Moralistics and Psychomoralistics. (The acronyms LAMP, MFT, CASE, and M&PM refer to these research programmes, respectively.) Then, I show how an emerging line of research related to developing a framework for a psychology of norms (Sripada and Stich 2007; Saunders 2009) can also be incorporated.

This unification assumes (at least) two systems of cognition, namely, System 1 and System 2 (Evans and Over 1996; Evans and Frankish 2009) and that the subject matter of the cognitive science of moral intuition are the biologically evolved structures, processes, inputs, and outputs associated with System 1. This project of unification does not include moral deliberation that may occur in System 2 (what many philosophers would characterise as the appropriate domain of moral deliberation). This unification is only concerned with moral intuitions, understood as moral judgements not arrived at via a process of conscious deliberation. The purpose of this project is to give a descriptive account of the cognitive systems and processes that give rise to the moral intuitions in the minds of humans.

This unification uses the 'tri-partite hypothesis' from cognitive science. As mentioned previously, Marr (1982, 24) characterised three levels – "at which an information-processing device must be understood before one can be said to have understood it completely" – with

DOI: 10.4324/9781003205746-2

reference to three sets of questions. This analysis considers the first two sets of questions/levels.

> The Computational Theory: What is the goal of the computation, why is it appropriate, and what is the logic of the strategy by which it can be carried out?
> Representation and algorithm: How can this computational theory be implemented? In particular, what is the representation for the input and output, and what is the algorithm for the transformation?

(1982, 24)

The goal of the computations at the heart of intuitive moral categorisation is social coordination, and these computations are implemented by a number of interacting algorithms. But, as the linguistic analogy in moral psychology implies, just as there are a number of different natural languages that facilitate human communication, there are a number of different moral languages that facilitate human social coordination. Thus, here it is assumed that all humans share a biologically evolved set of interacting algorithms, but these algorithms can be activated in different ways, having different configurations, hierarchical relations, and weightings in different social groups. For example, I assume there are algorithms that underwrite certain intuitive moral principles (e.g. a principle relating to harm) but within these principles are variable parameters, and variation in the parameter settings explain (to some extent) the variability of human moral intuitions (e.g. a parameter specifying the scope of the principle). Furthermore, the different principles may be arranged hierarchically in different orders within different humans. This explains the universality of the existence of moral intuition (in the general case) and the variability in the nature of particular instances of moral intuition (in any specific case) across different human societies.

The chapter ends with examples to illustrate how the moral intuitions are produced. Sex is centrally important in the biological evolution of sexually reproducing species and so it should be no surprise that sex is regulated by evolved moral intuitions. To illustrate how intuitions about the permissibility or impermissibility of sex may be produced, I use two examples. The first focuses on the role of the Westermarck mechanism (Westermarck 1891) in the context of the impermissibility of sex with other, now sexually mature, people with whom previously an individual grew up, and the second examines moral intuitions about marriage. The third example involves the apparent fact that slavery was considered moral permissibility in many cultures throughout human history. The unified cognitive science of moral intuition I advance in this book seeks to explain all moral intuitions (that were part of stable larger moral codes) that have occurred throughout human history. Moral intuitions about sex and slavery have been different at different times through human history, yet have been part of stable larger moral codes, so both are particularly powerful examples to use in this context.

## The Linguistic Analogy in Moral Psychology (LAMP)

Rawls (1973, 46) assumes that: "each person beyond a certain age and possessed of the requisite intellectual capacity develops a sense of justice under normal social circumstances." He wishes to identify the principles that generate this sense of justice, and he goes on to suggest that:

> A useful comparison here is with the problem of describing the sense of grammaticalness that we have for the sentences of our native language. In this case the aim is to characterize the ability to recognize well-formed sentences by formulating clearly expressed principles which make the same discriminations as the native speaker.
>
> (1973, 46)

Note that the principles he wishes to identify are not explicitly represented principles in the mind of individuals, but rather they correspond to the computational processes that produce grammatical sentences in each human competent in their native language (without that human consciously deliberating) and that the science of linguistics seeks to identify.[1]

Since the application of the analogy by Rawls, it has been taken up by other researchers including Hauser (2006); Dwyer (2007); Huebner, Dwyer, and Hauser (2009); Dwyer, Huebner, and Hauser (2010); and Mikhail (2011). The central idea is to identify insights from linguistics and apply those insights to moral psychology. The insights I draw on relate to the principles and parameters model (PPM) from linguistics. Before discussing the application of the PPM in the context of moral intuitions, I will first present the basics of the model, and here I draw on the work of Sripada (2008) and Mikhail (2011). Chomsky (1988) presented the PPM in linguistics. The idea is that there exists a universal grammar that is innate to all humans and this consists of a series of principles. The existence of this pan-human set of principles is said to explain the communalities that exist across all human languages. However, associated with each principle is one or more parameters. The parameters can come to be set in more than one setting, and importantly, the instantiated parameter settings are not innate. The instantiated parameter settings within any individual are determined by experience as the individual human undergoes linguistic development. The existence of experience-relative parameter settings is said to explain the differences that exist across all human languages. A standard example used to illustrate the model is 'head directionality' in a phrase. The 'head' of a phrase is contrasted with the 'complement.' The head of a phrase, for example, may be a verb or a noun. English is considered 'head initial,' while Japanese is considered 'head final.' This means that in English the head of a phrase comes before the complement, while in Japanese, the head of the phrase follows the complement. Proponents of the PPM claim that English and Japanese have different parameter setting associated with the 'head directionality' principle. To illustrate this, consider the location of the verb 'walk' (the head of the phrase) in the following two English sentences: 'Walk slowly down there.' And 'Down there slowly walk.' Other languages such as German do not display strong 'head directionality' and so, presumably, there is no parameter set within German for the 'head directionality' principle.

Building on Chomsky's original suggestion, a number of researchers have applied the PPM in moral psychology including (Stich 1993; Mikhail, Sorrentino, and Spelke 1998; Dwyer 1999; Harman 1999). The idea is that within the moral faculty there exist a number of principles, and these principles are universal across humanity. Associated with these principles are certain parameters and the settings of these parameters vary among humans. On this account, there is an innate capacity that is then modified by environmental factors (say, socio-cultural referencing), to produce a local competence in moral intuition. For example, Harman has suggested "there might be a universal principle containing a parameter G forbidding harm to members of G, where different moralities have different specifications for the relevant G." (2008, 348). So, one individual (within one socio-cultural context) may come to count all humans as members of group G, while another individual (within a different socio-cultural context) may come to count a particular subset of humans as members of G. But importantly, both will have achieved a local (i.e. socio-culturally relative) competence in moral intuition when that process is complete. The final aspect of the principles and parameters approach is a distinction drawn between competence and performance. While an individual who has undergone this process will have an ability to competently produce moral intuitions, they might not always succeed because of confounding factors. This distinction is assumed to be analogous to the competence/performance distinction in natural language. As I have mentioned above, I think the analogy with grammar needs to be re-framed.

But, to my mind, a number of principles and parameters understood as instantiated by computational algorithms (located at the central level in the 'tri-level hypothesis') is the way to understand the process that produces moral intuitions. Mikhail has done the most advanced work attempting to articulate the actual detail of the computational algorithms (2011). He has developed a series of algorithms that, he claims, produce results that correlate strongly with the answers of human subjects when they give intuitive responses to the moral permissibility or impermissibility of various options in 'trolley car' scenarios.[2] In particular, he has ranked, in order from permissible to impermissible, 11 variations of trolley car scenarios based on participants intuitive responses. And he has provided a detailed set of computational processes that, he claims, is the origin of these intuitions. More specifically, he uses structural descriptions, in the form of 'act trees,' that model the actual computations in human minds that lead to the production of moral intuitions. To make this point again, he is providing what he claims is the actual computational process that yield, within a person's System 1 processes, the intuitive moral judgements found in the empirical data. This is a bold claim, but it is, I believe, worth taking seriously.

The central principle of the algorithm is built around 'the doctrine of double effect' with reference to the permissibility or impermissibility of causing harm. This, of course, is only one principle relevant to moral intuition. There presumably will be more. But, if he is right, he is well on the way to identifying the cognitive principles that Rawls pointed to when he first proposed the linguistic analogy. Mikhail's work involves constructing computational algorithms that deal with a very tightly constrained set of circumstances (namely, trolley car scenarios), but the lessons learnt in his work can be applied in other contexts.

I assume that there will be a number of intuitive moral principles that will interact in some way, broadly analogous to the way a number of principles interact to produce our natural competence in language. Such research is in the very early stages, but there could be further higher-level principles that rank the priority of lower-level principles creating an ordering of the priority of lower-level principles. Or indeed, there may be higher-level principles that dictate whether lower-level principles are active or not. This may be the way to more fully understand the phenomenon explored by Haidt relating to the distinction between 'liberals' and 'conservatives' in US politics. The claim is that the moral intuitions of some people (identified as 'liberal' in the context of US politics) can be understood with reference to the functioning of two moral foundations, namely, harm/care and fairness/cheating, while the moral intuitions of other people (identified as 'conservative' in the context of US politics) can be understood with reference to the functioning of all of the moral foundations identified in Moral Foundations Theory (MFT) (Haidt 2012).

The application of the linguistic analogy assumes that there is a computational order to be identified in relation to the production of moral intuitions. However, the generation of moral intuitions may be much less ordered than proponents of LAMP assume. As I mentioned above, the generation of moral intuitions may be similar to the Pandemonium account of language generation discussed by Dennett so that the production of moral intuitions may involve "opportunistic, parallel, evolutionary processes – almost all the way down." (1991, 242). But I think the term 'Pandemonium' implies too little regularity. I assume that there is a significant level of regularity in the production of moral intuitions in any one person, such that reasonably stable patterns of moral intuitions emerge (from the moral grammar that any individual has internalised). In this book, I am (perhaps optimistically) assuming that the moral faculty would generate a computationally ordered set of moral intuitions. But, the set of systems that generate moral intuitions may not be operating in any coordinated sense at all, and it may just be the 'loudest' intuition among an uncoordinated group of intuitions that finds its way to consciousness, and is then labelled, by default, 'the' relevant moral intuition. Hopefully future research will shed light on this issue.

## Moral Foundations Theory (MFT)

MFT has emerged from work in moral psychology that rejects the idea, advanced by some, such as Kohlberg (1973), that there is one foundation for moral judgement, for example, universalisability. MFT assumes that there is more than one foundation (Fiske 1991; Shweder et al. 1997). MFT currently claims there are at least the following foundations for moral judgement: care/harm; fairness/cheating; loyalty/betrayal; authority/subversion; and sanctity/degradation (Graham et al. 2013), and Haidt further adds liberty/oppression (2012). However, proponents of MFT (Haidt and Joseph 2004, 2007; Graham et al. 2013) openly acknowledge that it is a developing research programme and so accept the future revision of these claims in the light of future research.

Furthermore, proponents of MFT endorse the following basic characteristics of moral psychology: (1) nativism, (2) cultural learning, (3) intuitionism, and (4) pluralism (Graham et al. 2013). Nativism is combined with cultural learning. The relation between these is illustrated with the metaphor of the drafting process of writing, whereby there is a first draft of the moral mind that is innate, and this first draft is then edited by cultural learning during psychological development. Prompted by the 'automaticity revolution' in social psychology (Bargh and Chartrand 1999), MFT assumes that moral judgements are intuitive judgements that are only supported by deliberative reasoning after the fact. And, MFT endorses the existence of multiple moral foundations that then lead to the production of a plurality of moral intuitions. Finally, proponents stress that they are engaged in a descriptive and not a normative project (Graham et al. 2013).

One of the most powerful examples articulated in the research that lead to MFT is the one involving a story read to participants in psychological experiments about Julie and Mark, a brother and sister, who decide to have consensual sex as adults while using two forms of birth control (Haidt 2001). When asked whether this was wrong, most participants in the experiments quickly report that it was wrong. But when asked to justify why they think it was wrong they are sometimes unable to provide a justification that is not called into question given the detail of the original story. This has been characterised as 'moral dumbfounding,' where people are said to have a clear moral intuition about a particular moral question but are unable to provide a justification that is not questionable (even with reference to their own moral deliberations). Examples such as this are offered as evidence that our moral intuitions are produced by a different system to the one that is producing our deliberative moral justifications.

I support the broad project of MFT as it is presented by its advocates. Additionally, and of central importance to the project advanced in this book, I claim that there is a natural alignment between LAMP and MFT. The moral foundations identified in MFT can be seen as the basic elements of a set of moral computational algorithms that I have described within my re-framing of LAMP. Thus, the moral foundations identified in MFT can be understood as the principles and parameters identified in LAMP. The principles in LAMP are the innate aspects of the moral foundations in MFT and the parameter settings from LAMP are set via the socio-cultural learning process identified in MFT. This is how I interpret the claim made by proponents of MFT that there is a drafting process during the development of the moral mind.

## Cognitive Adaptations for Social Exchange (CASE)

The next elements of the unifying account I wish to consider are Cognitive Adaptations for Social Exchange (CASE) as they are developed by Cosmides and Tooby (1992, 2015). I have suggested that LAMP and MFT can be combined to form the basis of a unified cognitive science of moral intuition. MFT identifies care/harm as one of the moral foundations and I have suggested that the work of Mikhail can be used as a model to illustrate how work can be done to uncover the detail of the actual computational algorithms generating moral intuitions about the permissibility or impermissibility of causing harm (mediated in Mikhail's work through the doctrine of double effect). But, care/harm is only one of the moral foundations identified by MFT. To advance a unified cognitive science of moral intuition, it will be necessary to provide detailed accounts of the computational algorithms at work in all of the moral foundations (accepting that the current list of foundations may change in the light of future research). The work of Cosmides and Tooby can serve as a second model to illustrate how future research can be conducted, their work being related to the fairness/cheating moral foundation in MFT.

So, to repeat these points for emphasis, I see the moral foundations identified in MFT as the basic elements of a set of moral computational algorithms that I have described within my re-framing of LAMP. I understand the moral foundations identified by MFT to be the principles and parameters identified in LAMP. I see the principles in LAMP as the innate aspects of the moral foundations in MFT and the parameter settings from LAMP are set via the socio-cultural learning process identified in MFT. Mikhail's work on harm/care and Cosmides and Tooby's work on fairness/cheating provide illustrations of how the detail of the principles and parameters are examined empirically.

Located within the broader evolutionary psychology research programme, Cosmides and Tooby's research is concerned with identifying 'social contract algorithms' characterised as neurocomputational systems "whose design features are adaptively specialised for producing the specific kinds of inferences and goals necessary to create cooperative interactions." (2008a, 53).

The algorithms manage social exchanges that essentially involve two features, 'rationed benefits', and 'requirements'. In Cosmides and Tooby's own words:

> Social exchange is cooperation for mutual benefit. If there is nothing in a conditional rule that can be interpreted as a rationed

benefit, then interpretive procedures should not categorize that rule as a social contract. To trigger the inference about obligations and entitlements that are appropriate to social contracts, the rule must be interpreted as restricting access to a benefit to those who have met a requirement. [...] Cheating is a specific way of violating a social contract. It is taking the benefit when you are not entitled to do so.

(2008a, 81)

Perhaps, the work of Cosmides and Tooby is most well known in relation to their experiments concerning social exchange versions of the Wason selection task (2008a, 79). In the selection task, the same logical problem (of testing a situation for the instantiation of a rule 'If P then Q') is presented to subjects in two contexts. Most subjects pick the correct answers when the problem is presented as a task of detecting a cheat in a social exchange context. But most subjects fail to pick the correct answers when the problem is presented in a neutral context. Cosmides and Tooby claim that the difference is explained by the fact that a cheat detection algorithm is activated in the social exchange context but not the neutral context. Cosmides and Tooby's work has been subject to criticism and for a sense of that debate see (Cosmides and Tooby 2008a, 2008b, 2008c; Fodor 2008; Mallon 2008), but I suggest that their work is uncovering the real nature of mental structures and processes that generate moral intuitions.

One could understand this in completely consciously deliberative terms. One could imagine two parties consciously and deliberatively entering into a social exchange agreement. One party sets a requirement, and on the assumption that the requirement is met by a second party, then a rationed benefit is provided by the first party to the second. Alternatively, one party may offer a rationed benefit to the second party conditional upon the second party meeting a requirement, and when the requirement is met, the rationed benefit is provided. This is, of course, the nature of legal contracts.

But, the subject matter of this book is not conscious and deliberative contracts. This book is about moral intuitions. So, what is relevant here is the possible existence of 'intuitive contracts' (understood as intuitive social exchange arrangements). And these intuitive contracts could have been constructed by cultural or social expectations that were never deliberatively considered or deliberately discussed by individuals. The idea here is that these intuitive contracts exist and thus there is a social expectation that they are honoured. When they are honoured, there is no related conflict, but when they are not honoured, there is related conflict. Or, if no explicit conflict is manifest, then perhaps intuitive moral judgements will occur that may lead to an emotional response such as 'righteous anger' associated with the failure to honour the intuitive contact. Finally, and importantly, there may be variation in the intuitive assumptions about what intuitive contracts are in force.

There are three situations worth highlighting here. Firstly, it may be the case that everyone in a culture intuitively knows what intuitive contracts are in force (in the language of principles and parameter settings, the settings are common across the culture). If everyone honours the intuitive contracts, then there is no conflict. But, it could be the case that even though everyone intuitively knows the contractual arrangement, some party to an intuitive contract may not honour that contract. So perhaps (even though both parties intuitively know the nature of the intuitive contract and have intuitively accepted the terms of that contract), one party provides the rationed benefit on the expectation that the requirement is met, but the requirement is not met. Or one party meets the requirement, but then the other party does not provide the rationed benefit. There are also other variations, for example, one pair of potential partners might enter an intuitive contract involving rationed benefits and corresponding requirements, but then one of the pair enters a different intuitive contract involving rationed benefits and requirements with a third party, and not surprisingly this will lead to conflict between the two people in the original paring because expectations have not been met.

Secondly, and more interestingly for the purposes of the current discussion, it may be the case that there is variation across the intuitions of individuals within a culture about whether certain intuitive social exchange contracts are taken to be in force at all (in the language of principles and parameter settings, the settings are not common across the culture). Some people in a culture may intuitively take certain things to always be rationed benefits, and therefore, there always exist corresponding requirements, while others may intuitively take these same things not necessarily to be rationed benefits and thus there are not always corresponding requirements in force.

And thirdly, it may be the case that everyone within one culture agrees about what intuitive contracts involving rationed benefits and requirements are in place, but that within another distinct culture there is a significantly different set of intuitive contracts in place (in the language of principles and parameters, the two cultures have distinct sets of parameter settings). This situation corresponds to the fact that these two cultures are using two distinct intuitive moral languages.

In the light of this brief review of their work, I hope that it is reasonably clear how the work of Cosmides and Tooby is a natural fit within the synthesis of LAMP and MFT. Their work is centrally concerned with providing the detail of how a computational algorithm can explain the human capacity to form moral intuitions about social exchange and when cheating is occurring within social exchange contexts. So, their work could be used as a model to provide the computational detail for the fairness/cheating moral algorithm (or algorithms) operating within the wider set of moral intuitions. The social exchange algorithm fits neatly within the principles and parameters model where all humans will recognise the potential for an intuitive social exchange contract to exist (the universal principle), but different human cultures will recognise different pairs of actual events or states of affairs as instantiating different rationed benefits and requirements (the varying parameter settings).

## A graphical representation of a combination of LAMP, MFT, and CASE

Now, I put all these together with the help of some graphical representations. Firstly, a version of linguistic theory assumes the existence of a language faculty that develops and functions as represented in Figure 2.1. Humans have an innate capacity to learn a language. This innate capacity in combination with experiences in the local linguistic environment yields competence in the local natural language. A human may use their natural language competently, but performance may fall below competence for reasons such as distraction, etc.

Secondly, a number of advocates of the linguistic analogy in moral psychology assume the existence of a moral faculty that develops

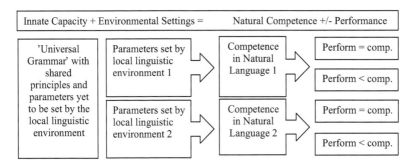

*Figure 2.1* The Principles and Parameters Model in Linguistics.

and functions as represented in Figure 2.2. Humans have an innate capacity to learn an intuitive 'moral language.' This innate capacity in combination with experiences in the local moral environment yields competence in the local moral language. A human may use their moral language competently, but performance may fall below competence for reasons such as distraction, etc.

Thirdly, proponents of MFT propose five or more moral foundations, including Harm/Care (H/C) and Fairness/Cheating (F/C). Figure 2.3 represents how LAMP, MFT, and CASE can be unified in M&PM. So, again, humans have an innate capacity to learn an intuitive 'moral language.' This innate capacity in combination with experiences in the local moral environment yields competence in the local moral language. The detail of the nature of local competence could be informed by Mikhail's work on permissible harm involving the 'doctrine of double effect' and Cosmides & Tooby's work on social exchange involving 'rationed benefits' and 'requirements.'

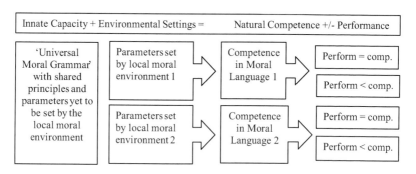

*Figure 2.2* The Principle and Parameters Model in LAMP.

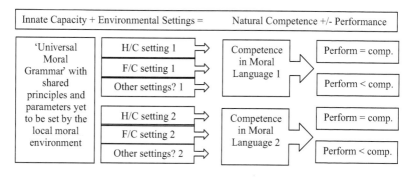

*Figure 2.3* Unifying LAMP, MFT, and CASE in M&PM.

And again, human may use their moral language competently, but performance may fall below competence for reasons such as distraction, etc.

## How this relates to work in social norms more broadly

Now, I turn to the issue of how the unified cognitive science of moral intuition I am advancing here relates to research seeking to understand social norms more broadly. There are a number of researchers who understand the structuring of social norms in terms of grammar including Richerson and Boyd (2005, 230) and Bicchieri (2006). A comprehensive discussion of all this research is beyond the scope of this book. But, there is one specific area of research, seeking to understand social norms, that I will discuss. Sripada and Stich offer a framework for the psychology of norms. Their goal is to offer "an account of the psychological mechanisms and processes underlying (social) norms that integrates what is known and can serve as a framework for future research" (2007, 280). They conceive of the psychological mechanisms and processes as broadly divided between an acquisition mechanism and an execution mechanism.

> The function of the acquisition mechanism is to identify behavioural cues indicating that a norm prevails in the local cultural environment, to infer the content of that norm, and to pass information about the content of the norm on to the implementation system, where it is stored and used.
>
> (2007, 289)

Within the execution mechanism, they identify a norm database and a rule-related reasoning capacity (2007, 298) and they note that one of the aims of a mature theory of the psychology of norms is to specify what can and cannot end up in that database (2007, 281).

My project to articulate a unified cognitive science of moral intuitions can be broadly understood as an attempt to answer the same questions that Sripada and Stich are addressing. But, while there are some similarities, there are some important differences between my position and the position of Sripada and Stich.

Firstly, I don't draw such a clear distinction between the acquisition mechanism and the execution mechanism. As illustrated in Figure 2.3, I think that an innate moral capacity in combination with social experiences in the local moral environment yields competence in the local 'moral language.' So, what Sripada and Stich think of as a norm database and rule-related reasoning capacity, I think of as an arrangement of algorithms that constitute (after relevant social experiences) an individual's intuitive moral language. So, I take it that Sripada and Stich are referring to the same cognitive system as I am, but they and I characterise the system differently.

Secondly, they make a distinction between a set of norms and a set of moral intuitions. As evidence of the fact that they think norms and moral intuitions are not co-extensive, they observe that

> the norm database, for many people in many cultures, will include lots of rules governing what food can be eaten, how to dispose of the dead, how to show deference to high-ranking people, and a host of other matters that our common-sense intuition does not count as moral.

(2007, 291)

But what counts as morally relevant in what has been insightfully called WEIRD (Western, Educated, Industrialised, Rich, and Democratic) culture by Henrich, Heine, and Norenzayan (2010) may only be a subset of what is considered morally relevant by other cultures. So, rather than taking these cultural differences to be a reason to distinguish between norms and moral intuitions, I see them as being produced by the same cognitive systems and processes. Note that within MFT these are exactly the types of things that are included in the moral foundations identified. Recall that the foundations include care/harm, fairness/cheating, loyalty/betrayal, authority/subversion, and sanctity/degradation (Graham et al. 2013). And, the proponents of MFT take variation across the activations and weighting of these foundations to explain why there is variation across cultures about what is or is not taken to be morally relevant.[3] And, in the terms of my project, the explanation is that different groups of humans simply use different moral languages.

Thirdly, another reason that Sripada and Stich (2007, 291) doubt that norms (i.e. the type in their norms database) and moral intuitions (the type that arise from within the systems and processes that I am discussing in this book) are not co-extensive is because of the so-called moral/conventional distinction (Turiel 1983).

Given the evolutionary assumptions I make in this book, there may be some way to understand the distinction between the moral and the conventional with reference to the distinction between what Sperber calls the 'proper domain' and the 'actual domain' of a system that has a 'biological function.' Here is how Sperber characterises these three concepts (and note that he is assuming the existence of 'conceptual modules' in this passage, but for our purposes, think of these simply as the systems involved in the production of moral intuitions):

> The actual domain of a conceptual module is all the information in the organism's environment that may (once processed by perceptual modules, and possibly by other conceptual modules) satisfy the module's input conditions. Its proper domain is all the information that it is the module's biological function to process. Very roughly, the function of a biological device is a class of effects of that device that contributes to making the device a stable feature of an enduring species. The function of a module is to process a specific range of information in a specific manner. That processing contributes to the reproductive success of the organism. The range of information that it is the function of a module to process constitutes its proper domain. What a module actually processes is information found in its actual domain, whether or not it also belongs to its proper domain.
>
> (1994, 51–52)

I assume that there is a biologically evolved faculty that generates moral intuitions, and so I assume this faculty has a biological function. Adapting the characterisation offered by Sperber '*the range of information that it is the function of the faculty generating moral intuitions to process constitutes its proper domain. What this faculty actually processes is information found in its actual domain, whether or not it also belongs to its proper domain.*' So, perhaps moral intuitions are outputs of this faculty associated with information in its proper domain, while intuitions about conventions are outputs of the moral faculty associated with information in its actual domain but not in its proper domain.

The work of Sripada and Stich (2007) articulating a framework for the psychology of norms has been taken further by Saunders (2009). Saunders is motivated by a worry that moral intuitions may not be respectable, he writes:

> Moral intuitions are the sorts of easy and immediate moral judgements that we constantly make without any conscious effort and that strike us with a perception like quality – characteristics that distinguish them from ordinary deductions that are comparatively slow and effortful. Moreover, unlike moral judgements in the deductive model, the sources of our moral intuitions are opaque, and we do not know what, if any, principles might underlie them.
>
> (2009, 335)

In particular, he is worried about moral dumbfounding: "dumbfounding strongly suggests then that the deductive model cannot explain the rational basis of moral intuition, and by extension, it casts doubt on the rationality of morality as a whole." (2009, 336)

This book is not concerned with the philosophical justification of any moral intuition. It is only concerned with a psychological description of the capacity to produce and consume moral intuitions. But Saunders concerns are informative here. He sees a problem in the role of moral intuition in moral judgement. This is a good way of illustrating the relationship between my project and moral philosophy. In my view, Saunders has correctly identified the fact that System 1 produces moral intuitions and System 2 produces moral deliberation. Saunders wants one's moral intuitions to align with the outputs of one's moral deliberations. And, he suggests this is possible by System 2 educating System 1.

In the language of my project, Saunders is suggesting a person may choose to learn a new intuitive moral language. And, indeed, it may be possible to learn a new intuitive moral language. But, some very interesting research questions emerge here. Just how does a person deliberately learn a new intuitive moral language? Once deliberatively learnt (if that is possible), do the two intuitive moral languages remain distinct? Or is there some interaction between them? Does one overwrite the other? These are all important questions.[4] But at this point in the development of the research programme I am seeking to advance there is a lot of work to be done simply to identify how any intuitive moral language is learnt at all. Research relating to deliberatively learning a second intuitive moral language is a research project a little bit further down the track.

## Examples of moral intuitions at work

I now illustrate the unification pursued in this chapter with a number of examples. As I have said, I assume that the systems and processes that produce moral intuitions have deep evolutionary origins. I further assume that in the most recent past of the human species, by which I mean at least all recorded human history, there has been insufficient time for these systems and processes to undergo any significant biological evolution. This implies that the sets of moral intuitions generated by groups of humans throughout history have been produced by the same cognitive systems and processes. A consequence of this is that all well-established moral systems through human history (that were built up out of a shared set of moral intuitions) should be understandable using the resources of the unified cognitive science of moral intuition. More specifically, I assume some stability and some variability as follows: (1) the classes of principles are stable, for example, these might be reasonably well characterised by work in MFT such that there is one (or possibly more) principles focused specifically on such things as harm/care and fairness/cheating, etc.; (2) the principles themselves are stable, for example, a stable principle might be that harming members of group G is impermissible, as has been suggested by Harman (2008, 347), or "If you accept a benefit from agent X, then you must satisfy X's requirement" (Cosmides and Tooby 2008a, 72); but in contrast to the stability of both the classes of principle and the nature of the principles themselves, (3) the parameter settings within the principles vary across intuitive moral languages; and (4) the hierarchical relations that may exist between principles may also vary across intuitive moral languages.

I will use a number of examples in the hope of demonstrating how the unified cognitive science of moral intuition can be used to understand the breadth of moral intuitions that have been produced over the time in which we have reliable records of the various moral intuitions produced by humans.

These examples involve a range of moral intuitions that people today may not share. But the point of this analysis is not only to demonstrate how the moral intuitions being produced today can be understood, but rather it is to demonstrate how moral intuitions that have been produced throughout human history can be understood. And I note again that this book is not concerned with moral deliberation (that is produced by System 2), so I won't be examining what outputs System 2 might produce about the issues discussed below.

The first two examples relate to sex. Our evolutionary ancestors have been reproducing sexually for around 2 billion years and obviously sex is important to any sexually reproducing species. So, it is not surprising that sex became a central subject of moral intuitions when the production of such intuitions emerged in our evolutionary lineage.

The first example involving sex is incest avoidance. As has been discussed above, Haidt (2001) recounts research in which participants are asked to comment on the morality of the consensual sex between a brother and sister, Mark and Julie. Researchers found that participants often had a clear intuition that it was wrong but could not necessarily offer a reflectively sustainable justification for that intuition. This suggests to some that the judgement is an intuitive one.

From an evolutionary perspective, incest avoidance may be significant enough that natural selection has resulted in cognitive systems that generate intuitive judgements of avoidance (perhaps accompanied by a negative emotional affect) when triggered in a particular way, as was suggested by Westermarck (1891). Consider an adult contemplating having sex with another adult when those two people grew up together in the same family. This appears to be sufficient to trigger the judgement of avoidance, even when the two people are not biological siblings (Barrett, Dunbar, and Lycett 2002, 222). So, in terms of the systems and processes that produce moral intuitions, there may be a principle 'Don't have sex with other adults in Group S.' And the membership of Group S (the parameter settings of the principle) is set by two or more adult's experiences of growing up together in the same family in childhood.

Such a mechanism would suggest that individuals in all human cultures would have the intuition (emerging at some point of in their psychological development) not to have sex with those with whom they spent their childhood growing up in the same family. Historical examples of sibling incest in the royal families of Egypt, Peru, and Hawaii have been offered as counterexamples, and these counterexamples need to be seriously considered. But not everyone is convinced by them (Bixler 1982). The existence of these counterexamples does not necessarily demonstrate that the moral intuition to avoid incest does not exist, but only that if the moral intuition does exist, it does not have an action-guiding role in particular circumstances. This is consistent with the ideas presented in this book, simply because another moral intuition, perhaps based on loyalty or authority might be the action-guiding intuition in such cases. Alternatively, incest in royal families might have been motivated by pragmatic factors completely unrelated to any moral intuitions.

The second example involving sex focuses on sexual selection (as distinct from natural selection) and examines female mate choice and its relationship to the concept of sex as a 'rationed benefit' and what has been called 'sexual economics' (Baumeister and Vohs 2004). Sexual selection involves the interactions between male–male competition and female mate choice (Hunt et al. 2008). But why do females choose their mates, and males compete with other males? From an evolutionary perspective, the choices females make in relation to having sex with mates involve exploiting the reproductive potential and reproductive investment of the mate. "Reproductive potential is defined as the genetic, material, and/or social resources an individual can invest in offspring, and reproductive investment is the actual use of these resources to enhance the physical and social well-being of offspring" (Geary, Vigil, and Byrd-Craven 2004, 27).

The answer to the question "why do females choose, and males compete?" to a large extent, is provided by the different levels of reproductive investment provided by males and females.

> The sex that provides more than his or her share of parental investment becomes, in effect, an important reproductive resource for members of the opposite sex [...] One result is competition among members of the lower investing sex (typically males) over the parental investment of members of the higher investing sex (typically females). Members of the higher investing sex are thus in demand and can be choosy when it comes to mates.
>
> (Geary, Vigil, and Byrd-Craven 2004, 27)

This characterisation of females being in demand suggests that sex itself can be understood as a rationed benefit that is exchanged for the actual investment by males of their reproductive potential in their offspring. This characterisation is consistent with what is known as 'sexual economics,' a theoretical approach that understands sex as a female resource for social exchange (Baumeister and Vohs 2004).

I suggest all this fits well into CASE. As explained above, CASE assumes that a social exchange involves a rationed benefit and a requirement. And the assumption is that one of the contracting pair in the social exchange will provide a rationed benefit in exchange for a requirement. But if the requirement is not met, then the rationed benefit is withheld. Assuming that the provision of sex by a female is a rationed benefit, then a requirement could very plausibly be for a male to actually invest their reproductive potential in the offspring of the pair.

Although I am not aware of Cosmides and Tooby framing this contractual agreement in terms of the principles and parameters model I am advancing here, they do offer the following rule that can be interpreted as a principle: "If you accept a benefit from agent X, then you must satisfy X's requirement." (2008a, 72). That rule can be understood as a principle. The next questions are: what is a rationed benefit and what is the associated requirement in any particular instantiation of this principle? And the answers can be defined by parameter settings associated with the principle.

It may be the case that all humans intuitively consider the provision of sex by females as the provision of a rationed benefit and that there is an intuitive requirement that males actually invest their reproductive potential in the offspring of any pairing. This would be in line with the sexual selection that exists within other animals. But it is also possible that some humans (in some societies) do not intuitively consider the provision of sex by females as a rationed benefit.

Indeed, the analysis I am advancing in this book allows for the possibility that within some intuitive moralities sex is a rationed benefit and in others it is not. But if the general idea I am advancing is correct, then presumably all human intuitive moralities include the principle: "If you accept a benefit from agent X, then you must satisfy X's requirement." (Cosmides and Tooby 2008a, 72) even though when this principle is active would vary across human intuitive moralities.

Consider the possibility that the provision of sex by females is a rationed benefit and the associated requirement is that males accepting the benefit are required to actually invest their reproductive potential in offspring of the pair. This may contribute to possible explanations of a number of moral intuitions relating to marriage, for example, the historically common intuition (and its expression in culture) concerning the impermissibly of sex before marriage, and indeed the existence of the institution of marriage itself, as illustrated by the following observation:

> One solution to the puzzle of why men would seek marriage comes from the ground rules set by women. Because it is clear that many ancestral women required reliable signs of male commitment before consenting to sex, men who failed to commit would have suffered selectively on the mating market. Men who failed to show interest in commitment might have failed to attract any women at all.[5]
>
> (Buss 2009, 139)

For discussions of these themes within the specific context of 'sexual economics,' see Baumeister and Vohs (2004) and Rudman and Fetterolf (2014) and within the broader context of the 'cultural suppression of female sexuality,' see Baumeister and Twenge (2002).

The final example I will use is slavery. There is evidence of slavery from the very earliest times in recorded history, for example, slaves are referred to multiple times in the Code of Hammurabi (1750 BC). The way that slaves are referred to in the code indicates that slavery was legally permissible, and I will assume that it can be reasonably inferred from that that slavery was considered intuitively morally permissible as well.

Furthermore, Aristotle, in Book 1 Chapter Five of Politics (2009), offers a justification of slavery, so I will assume that he also considered slavery to be intuitively morally permissible. Although these texts don't give us access to the actual moral intuitions that people experienced at the time, I will assume here that this textual evidence is sufficient to demonstrate that people considered slavery to be intuitively morally permissible.

The unified cognitive science of moral intuition that I advance in the book should be able to account for all historically recorded human moral codes (that are based on intuitive moral reasoning). Thus, the account I provide should be able to accommodate the moral intuitions being produced in the minds of the people of Babylon and ancient Greece, who found slavery morally permissible, as well as accommodate the intuitions of people today who find slavery morally impermissible. I suggest this can be done with the resources available within the unified cognitive science of moral intuition presented here.

First, consider Harman's contribution. As I have mentioned, Harman suggests that "there might be a universal principle containing a parameter G forbidding harm to members of G, where different moralities have different specifications of the relevant G." (2008, 347). So, for the sake of the current argument, assume that there is a principle as follows: 'harming members of group G is impermissible,' and further assume that for the humans throughout history who have had the moral intuition that slavery was permissible, these humans did not consider slaves to be members of group G. Then, it may be the case that these people had the following intuitions:

Enslaving members of group G is a harm and is impermissible (because it is a harm), but enslaving non-members of G is permissible (because they are not members of G).

This appears to be reasonably consistent with Aristotle's justification of slavery, although given he has a distinct category of 'natural slaves' a more accurate analysis may involve what is permissible and impermissible with respect to his (perhaps intuitive) understanding of the group 'natural slaves' (2009).

In this context, it is worth mentioning that within his own work Mikhail assumes that the algorithm that judges the permissibility or impermissibility of harm involves the core assumption that "the life of one person has the same moral worth as that of another" (2011, 139). If Mikhail's assumption is to be understood as the parameter setting that all humans are members of group G, and assuming slavery is a harm then presumably (*pace* Aristotle) enslaving any human is impermissible. But, as noted above, that is not the only parameter setting available.

Now, I understand all these are 'high stakes' examples. But, as pointed out by Harman, perhaps it is only by considering what he calls "hard cases" that the principles and parameters will be identified (2008, 350). And I do not assume that I have done enough here to offer a comprehensive account of how the principles and parameters settings explain the production of moral intuitions in these examples. All I hope to have provided is a prompt for some interesting lines of research to be pursued within a unified cognitive science of moral intuition.

## Summary of chapter

Using a re-framed Linguistic Analogy in Moral Psychology (incorporating the 'tri-level hypothesis' from cognitive science), I have suggested that existing work from Moral Foundations Theory and Cognitive Adaptations for Social Exchange can be combined with emerging work identifying a Framework for the Psychology of Norms to form a unified cognitive science of moral intuition.

## Notes

1   In more technical terms, Rawls is pointing to the computational processes that constitute a human's competency in "I-grammar" (Roedder and Harman 2010, 276).
2   So called 'trolley car' scenarios are used in thought experiments to elicit moral intuitions, and involve an imagined track down which a trolley car is moving without anyone on-board able to stop it. In the standard case the trolley car is heading toward a fork in the track. Down each fork in the track there are standing different numbers of people, for example, down the track the trolley is heading (if nothing is done) there may be five people working, but on the other track there may be 1 person working. The implication being that if (something is done and) the trolley is diverted to the other track 1 person will be killed rather than five people. The experimental subject is asked to imagine themselves in various situations in which they can affect the outcome, for example by diverting the trolley onto another track. The experiment involves asking experimental participants to judge whether or not certain actions (or lack of action) are morally impermissible, or obligatory, etc.
3   Other work relevant to this point is has been undertaken by Haidt, Koller, and Dias (1993), but see De Villiers-Botha (2020) for an alternative view.
4   Another important dimension of future research involves the question: how far does the analogy with language extend and where do disanalogies between language and intuitive morality exist?
5   More generally, it may contribute to the explanation of the intuitive moral approval by their female reproductive mates of male sexual fidelity and of the intuitive moral disapproval by their female reproductive mates of male sexual infidelity. This might even be relevant to intuitive moral disapproval (where it exists) of the use of pornography by males (as presumably

the evolved systems generating these intuitions are not capable of discriminating between actual infidelity and what might be called virtual infidelity). If a male uses pornography, then this undermines the 'rationed' nature of the benefit that females are offering males in the social exchange. Although, it should be noted that there are other relevant contributing factors that would need to be taken into account in any such explanations, including such things as evolutionary explanations of sexual jealousy (Barrett, Dunbar, and Lycett 2002, 182).

# References

Aristotle. 2009. "Politics: A Treatise on Government." In *The Project Gutenberg EBook of Politics*. The Project Gutenberg. https://www.gutenberg.org/files/6762/6762-h/6762-h.htm

Bargh, John A., and Tanya L. Chartrand. 1999. "The Unbearable Automaticity of Being." *American Psychologist* 54 (7):462–479.

Barrett, Louise, Robin Dunbar, and John Lycett. 2002. *Human Evolutionary Psychology*. Princeton: Princeton University Press.

Baumeister, Roy F., and Jean M. Twenge. 2002. "Cultural Suppression of Female Sexuality." *Review of General Psychology* 6 (2):166–203.

Baumeister, Roy F., and Kathleen D. Vohs. 2004. "Sexual Economics: Sex as Female Resource for Social Exchange in Heterosexual Interactions." *Personality and Social Psychology Review* 8 (4):339–363.

Bicchieri, Cristina. 2006. *The Grammar of Society: The Nature and Dynamics of Social Norms*. Cambridge: Cambridge University Press.

Bixler, Ray H. 1982. "Sibling Incest in the Royal Families of Egypt, Peru, and Hawaii." *Journal of Sex Research* 18 (3):264–281.

Buss, David M. 2009. *Evolutionary Psychology: The New Science of the Mind*. Boston, MA: Pearson.

Chomsky, Noam. 1988. *Language and Problems of Knowledge*. Cambridge, MA: MIT Press.

Cosmides, Leda, and John Tooby. 1992. "Cognitive Adaptations for Social Exchange." In *The Adapted Mind: Evolutionary Psychology and the Generation of Culture*, edited by Jerome Barkow, Leda Cosmides and John Tooby, 163–228. New York: Oxford University Press.

Cosmides, Leda, and John Tooby. 2008a. "Can a General Deontic Logic Capture the Facts of Human Moral Reasoning? How the Mind Interprets Social Exchange Rules and Detects Cheaters." In *Moral Psychology Volume 1: The Evolution of Morality: Adaptations and Innateness*, edited by Walter Sinnott-Armstrong, 53–119. Cambridge, MA: MIT Press.

Cosmides, Leda, and John Tooby. 2008b. "Can Evolutionary Psychology Assist Logicians? A Reply to Mallon." In *Moral Psychology Volume 1 The Evolution of Morality: Adaptations and Innateness*, edited by Walter Sinnott-Armstrong, 131–136. Cambridge, MA: MIT Press.

Cosmides, Leda, and John Tooby. 2008c. "When Falsification Strikes: A Reply to Fodor." In *Moral Psychology Volume 1 The Evolution of*

*Morality: Adaptations and Innateness*, edited by Walter Sinnott-Armstrong, 143–164. Cambridge, MA: MIT Press.

Cosmides, Leda, and John Tooby. 2015. "Adaptations for Reasoning About Social Exchange." In *The Handbook of Evolutionary Psychology*, edited by David M. Buss, 625–668. Hoboken, NJ: John Wiley & Sons.

De Villiers-Botha, Tanya. 2020. "Haidt et al.'s Case for Moral Pluralism Revisited." *Philosophical Psychology* 33 (2):244–261.

Dennett, Daniel. 1991. *Consciousness Explained.* London: Penguin.

Dwyer, Susan. 1999. "Moral Competence." In *Philosophy and linguistics*, edited by K. Murasugi and R. Stainton, 169–190. Boulder, CO: Westview Press.

Dwyer, Susan. 2007. "How Good is the Linguistic Analogy?" In The Innate Mind: Volume 2: Culture and Cognition, edited by Peter Carruthers, Stephen Laurence and Stephen Stich, 237–256. Oxford: Oxford University Press.

Dwyer, Susan, Bryce Huebner, and Marc D. Hauser. 2010. "The Linguistic Analogy: Motivations, Results, and Speculations." *Topics in Cognitive Science* 2:486–510.

Evans, Jonathan St. B. T., and Keith Frankish. 2009. *In Two Minds: Dual Processes and Beyond.* Oxford: Oxford University Press.

Evans, Jonathan St. B. T., and David E. Over. 1996. *Rationality and Reasoning.* Hove, UK: Psychology Press.

Fiske, A. P. 1991. *Structures of Social Life: The Four Elementary Forms of Social Relations: Communal Sharing, Authority Ranking, Equality Matching, Market Pricing.* New York: Free Press.

Fodor, Jerry. 2008. "Comment on Cosmides and Tooby." In *Moral Psychology Volume 1 The Evolution of Morality: Adaptation and Innateness*, edited by Walter Sinnott-Armstrong, 137–141. Cambridge: MIT Press.

Geary, David C., Jacob Vigil, and Byrd-Craven. 2004. "Evolution of Human Mate Choice." *Journal of Sex Research* 41 (1):27–42.

Graham, Jesse, Jonathan Haidt, Sena Koleva, Matt Motyl, Ravi Iyer, Sean Wojcik, and Peter Ditto. 2013. "Moral Foundations Theory: The Pragmatic Validity of Moral Pluralism." *Advances in Experimental Social Psychology* 47:55–130.

Haidt, Jonathan. 2001. "The Emotional Dog and Its Rational Tail: A Social Intuitionist Approach to Moral Judgment." *Psychological Review* 108 (4):814–834.

Haidt, Jonathan. 2012. *The Righteous Mind: Why Good People Are Divided by Politics and Religion.* London: Penguin.

Haidt, Jonathan, and Craig Joseph. 2004. "Intuitive Ethics: How Innately Prepared Intuitions Generate Culturally Variable Virtues." *Daedalus* 133:55–66.

Haidt, Jonathan, and Craig Joseph. 2007. "The Moral Mind: How Five Sets of Innate Intuitions Guide Development of Many Culture-Specific Virtues, and Perhaps Even Modules." In *The Innate Mind: Volume 3 Foundations and the Future*, edited by Peter Carruthers, Stephen Laurence and Stephen Stich, 367–392. Oxford: Oxford University Press.

Haidt, Jonathan, Silvia Helena Koller, and Maria G. Dias. 1993. "Affect, Culture, and Morality, or Is It Wrong to Eat Your Dog?" *Journal of Personality and Social Psychology* 65 (4):613–628.

Hammurabi. 1750 BC. "The Code of Hammurabi." Translated by L. W. King. In *The Avalon Project: Documents in Law, History and Diplomacy*. Yale Law School. https://avalon.law.yale.edu/ancient/hamframe.asp

Harman, Gilbert H. 1999. "Moral Philosophy and Linguistics." In Klaus Brinkman (ed.), Proceedings of the 20th World Congress of Philosophy: Volume I: Ethics, 107–115. Charlottesville, VA: Philosophy Documentation Center.

Harman, Gilbert H. 2008. "Using a Linguistic Analogy to Study Morality." In *Moral Psychology Volume 1: The Evolution of Morality: Adaptations and Innateness*, edited by Walter Sinnott-Armstrong, 345–352. Cambridge: MIT Press.

Hauser, Marc D. 2006. *Moral Minds: How Nature Designed Our Universal Sense of Right and Wrong*. New York: HarperCollins.

Henrich, Joseph, Steven J. Heine, and Ara Norenzayan. 2010. "The Weirdest People in the World?" *Behavioral and Brain Sciences* 33:61–135.

Huebner, Bryce, Susan Dwyer, and Marc D. Hauser. 2009. "The Role of Emotion in Moral Psychology." *Trends in Cognitive Science* 13 (1), 1–6.

Hunt, John, Casper J. Breuker, Jennifer A. Sadowski, and Allen J. Moore. 2008. "Male-Male Competition, Female Mate Choice and Their Interaction: Determining Total Sexual Selection." *Journal of Evolutionary Biology* 22:13–26.

Kohlberg, Lawrence. 1973. "The Claim to Moral Adequacy of a Highest Stage of Moral Development." The Journal of Philosophy 70:630–646.

Mallon, Ron. 2008. "Ought We to Abandon a Domain-General Treatment of "Ought"?" In *Moral Psychology Volume 1 The Evolution of Morality: Adaptations and Innateness*, edited by Walter Sinnott-Armstrong, 121–130. Cambridge: MIT Press.

Mikhail, John. 2011. *Elements of Moral Cognition: Rawl's Linguistic Analogy and the Cognitive Science of Moral and Legal Judgment*. Cambridge: Cambridge University Press.

Mikhail, John, Cristina Sorrentino, and Elizabeth Spelke. 1998. "Toward a Universal Moral Grammar." In Morton Ann Gernsbacher and Sharon J. Derry (eds), *Twentieth Annual Conference of the Cognitive Science Society*, 1250–1250. New York: Routledge.

Rawls, John. 1973. *A Theory of Justice*. Oxford: Oxford University Press.

Richerson, P. J., and R. Boyd. 2005. *Not by Genes Alone: How Culture Transformed Human Evolution*. Chicago: University of Chicago Press.

Roedder, Erica, and Gilbert H. Harman. 2010. "Linguistics and Moral Theory." In The Moral Psychology Handbook, edited by John Doris, 273–296. Oxford: Oxford University Press.

Rudman, Laurie A., and Janell C. Fetterolf. 2014. "Gender and Sexual Economics: Do Women View Sex as a Female Commodity?" *Psychological Science* 25 (7):1438–1447.

Saunders, Leland F. 2009. "Reason and Intuition in the Moral Life: A Dual-Process Account of Moral Justification." In *In Two Minds: Dual Processes and beyond*, edited by Jonathan St. B. T. Evans and Keith Frankish, 335–354. Oxford: Oxford University Press.

Shweder, R. A., N. C. Much, M. Mahapatra, and L. Park. 1997. "The "Big Three" of Morality (Autonomy, Community, Divinity) and the "Big Three" Explanations of Suffering." In *Morality and Health*, edited by A. M. Brandt and P. Rozin, 119–169. New York: Routledge.

Sperber, Dan. 1994. "The Modularity of Thought and Epidemiology of Representation." In *Mapping the Mind*, edited by L. Hirschfeld and S. Gelman, 39–67. Cambridge: Cambridge University Press.

Sripada, Chandra Sekhar. 2008. "Nativism and Moral Psychology: Three Models of the Innate Structure That Shapes the Content of Moral Norms." In *Moral Psychology Volume 1: The Evolution of Morality: Adaptations and Innateness*, edited by Walter Sinnott-Armstrong, 319–343. Cambridge: MIT Press.

Sripada, Chandra Sekhar, and Stephen Stich. 2007. "A Framework for the Psychology of Norms." In *The Innate Mind: Volume 2: Culture and Cognition*, edited by Peter Carruthers, Stephen Laurence and Stephen Stich, 280–301, New York: Oxford University Press.

Stich, Stephen. 1993. "Moral Philosophy and Mental Representation." In *The Origins of Values*, edited by M. Hechter, L. Nadel and R. Michod, 215–228. New York: Aldine de Gruyter.

Turiel, Elliot. 1983. *The Development of Social Knowledge*. Cambridge: Cambridge University Press.

Westermarck, E. A. 1891. *The History of Human Marriage*. New York: Macmillan.

# 3 Introducing Moralistics and Psychomoralistics

## Introducing the elephant

In this chapter, I present a re-framing of the Linguistic Analogy in Moral Psychology (LAMP) research programme, which I am calling Moralistics and Psychomoralistics (M&PM), in the hope it becomes a progressive scientific research programme, in the sense Lakatos used the term (1968). This project is a descriptive project about moral intuitions within moral psychology not a normative project within moral philosophy. I assume that there are cognitive structures, systems and processes that are responsible for the human capacity for moral intuition that are directly analogous to the cognitive structures, systems, and processes responsible for natural language. I suggest research in M&PM proceed as follows: identify a term and its referent from within Linguistics and Psycholinguistics, assume that an analogous referent exists, and then begin scientific research to test whether it exists, and, if it exists, to uncover the nature of the referent.[1] Humans have the capacity to recognise 'linguistically relevant elements' in their environment, understood as words and sentences in their spoken language. I suggest, analogously, humans have the capacity to recognise 'morally relevant elements' (that I call 'mords') within 'morally relevant contexts' (that I call 'mentences') in their intuitive moral language. The chapter ends with existing work from other researchers employing LAMP being reinterpreted within the reframed linguistic analogy presented here as M&PM.

## The Linguistic Analogy in Moral Psychology as it has been drawn to date

Here is how Rawls originally presents the linguistic analogy:

> Let us assume that each person beyond a certain age and possessed of the requisite intellectual capacity develops a sense of justice

DOI: 10.4324/9781003205746-3

under normal social circumstances. We acquire a skill in judging things to be just and unjust, and in supporting these judgments by reasons. ... Only a deceptive familiarity with our everyday judgments and our natural readiness to make them could conceal the fact that characterising our moral capacities is an intricate task. The principles which describe them must be presumed to have a complex structure, and the concepts involved will require serious study. ... A useful comparison here is with the problem of describing the sense of grammaticalness that we have for the sentences of our native language. In this case the aim is to characterize the ability to recognize well-formed sentences by formulating clearly expressed principles which make the same discriminations as the native speaker.

(1973, 46)

I believe Rawls is correctly identifying a central feature of intuitive moral cognition. But, let me re-present what he says within the framework I put forward in this book. The distinction between System 1 (intuitive reasoning) and System 2 (deliberative reasoning) helps identify what Rawls is pointing to here. In the passage above, Rawls describes an individual as having a 'sense of justice' that is constituted by 'a skill in judging things to be just and unjust.' This, I claim, is referring to the output of System 1 (intuitive moral reasoning). And Rawls' use of the terms 'sense' and 'skill' aligns with Kahneman's insight about the outputs of System 1 being located between the automatic operations of perception and the deliberate operations of reasoning (2002, 450). Furthermore, Rawls explicitly contrasts the sense of justice produced by 'a skill in judging things to be just or unjust' with 'reasons.' And when he says individuals support (their intuitive) judgements with reasons, he is pointing to the interaction between System 1 and System 2 that he himself characterises (although not in terms of System 1 & 2) as reflective equilibrium (1973). And it is worth noting in passing that this interaction between System 1 and System 2 is centrally relevant to the work being done by Saunders (2009) that was reviewed in the previous chapter.

Since Rawls' own application of the linguistic analogy, others have seen the value of it. Here is one example of how people understand the value of the analogy:

Inspired by the success of generative linguistics and transformational grammar, proponents of the linguistic analogy (LA) in moral psychology hypothesize that careful attention to folk-moral judgments is likely to reveal a small set of implicit rules and structures responsible for the ubiquitous and apparently unbounded capacity for making moral judgments. As a theoretical hypothesis, LA thus requires a rich description of the computational structures that underlie mature moral judgments, an account of the acquisition and development of these structures, and an analysis of those components of the moral system that are uniquely human and uniquely moral.

(Dwyer, Huebner, and Hauser 2010, 486)

Although I don't think that intuitive morality is uniquely human, this passage is one of the best characterisations of the way the linguistic analogy research programme should be understood. Furthermore, the most advanced application of the linguistic analogy has been developed by Mikhail (2011), and his work is a good example of how the characterisation of the research programme by Dwyer, Huebner, and Hauser (above) should be operationalised. Mikhail's project is to provide structural descriptions (in the form of 'act trees') that correctly model the actual computations in human minds that lead to the production of moral intuitions. He uses a series of trolley car scenarios, and he claims the set of different computational outputs generated by the structural descriptions he has offered, accurately map onto empirical data produced by testing human intuitions about the same series of trolley car scenarios. Whether he has identified the actual computations that produce the human intuitions in the trolley car scenarios is not the central point I want to emphasise here. My point is that Mikhail's work exemplifies how good work is being done by employing LAMP. And while good work continues to be done by researchers using the linguistic analogy, I believe a significant obstacle to further advances is the misunderstanding about what exactly the analogy amounts to. So, here, I offer a re-framing of the analogy.

### Introducing some Moralistics and Psychomoralistics research questions

One way of understanding how research in both M&PM could proceed is simply by assuming that there are certain cognitive structures, systems, and processes that constitute the human capacity for moral intuition that are analogous to the cognitive structures, systems, and processes that constitute the human capacity for natural language. In the terminology provided by Lakatos (1974), this is the 'hard core' of the scientific research programme.[2] And, Mikhail's work serves as a model of how such research is done. Some questions arising from the application of this analogy are presented in Table 3.1. I suggest research in M&PM proceed as follows. Identify a term and its referent from within Linguistics and Psycholinguistics and assume that an analogous referent exists (identified by a term in M&PM) and then begin scientific research that will (1) test whether it exists, and then if it exists, (2) uncover the nature of the referent. I am not an empirical scientist, but with reference to any empirical test or series of empirical tests, presumably the actual process might involve a null hypothesis that some cognitive structure or process does not exist and then would involve tests that may or may not lead to the rejection of the null hypothesis.

There are many more possible questions beyond those listed in Table 3.1. Table 3.1 merely lists the questions that I have thought about enough to offer what I take to be plausible answers. I invite others to pose and offer answers to other questions, or, indeed, offer different answers to these questions. To start the research ball rolling, I will now present my answers to the questions in Table 3.1. And because I am no expert in Linguistics and Psycholinguistics, here I rely on a standard textbook presentation (Harley 2014).

**What is the moralistic equivalent to language?**

Harley (2014, 5) answers, the question 'what is language?' as follows:

> a simple definition might be that it is 'a system of symbols and rules that enable us to communicate.' Symbols are things that stand for other things: Words, either written or spoken, are symbols. The rules specify how words are ordered to form sentences.

*Table 3.1* Questions Relating to Possible Analogues

| Linguistic Terms | Questions About Equivalent Moralistic Terms |
| --- | --- |
| Language | What is the moralistic equivalent of language? |
| Words | What is the moralistic equivalent of words (call them 'mords')? |
| Sentences | What is the moralistic equivalent of sentences (call them 'mentences')? |
| Syntax | What is the moralistic equivalent of syntax? |
| Semantics | What is the moralistic equivalent of semantics? |
| Pragmatics | What is the moralistic equivalent of pragmatics? |

By applying the analogy directly, we can ask: what are moral intuitions? Strictly speaking, a more accurate, but more convoluted question to ask would be: what are the systems of intuitive moral categorisation? But I will stay with the question: what are moral intuitions? And an analogical reconstrual of Harley's definition of language yields: moral intuitions are a system of symbols and rules that enable us to coordinate socially (where 'social coordination' is understood in a very broad sense). The rules in this case are the computations that researchers like Mikhail are attempting to identify. But what is the analogue to symbols here? What is functioning as a symbol in Moralistics? This is an important question and needs careful consideration. Indeed, I think failing to understand the answer to this question might be why many people fail to see the value of the original analogy Rawls was pointing to. Here is my answer.

Let me begin with natural language, and I set aside the written versions of natural language and focus only on sounds. Some sounds are recognised as words in our native language and other sounds are not. Here, I take the sounds that are recognised as words in our native language to no longer be merely sounds but now to be symbols. Recall Fodor's (1983, 56) insight about our inability to not hear a sentence in our native language as a sentence in our native language. Put slightly differently, it is impossible for us not to hear words in our native language as words in our native language. I take this mandatoriness to be central to symbols being symbols in my analysis. And I suggest that analogously, it is impossible for us not to see a pattern/bundle/set of morally relevant elements as a pattern/bundle/set of morally relevant elements when they have that status in our intuitive morality.[3]

Consider some set of features of the world. One person may recognise that set of features of the world as a morally relevant element. This is the equivalent of hearing a word in one's own language. But another person may not recognise that set of features of the world as morally relevant. This is equivalent of simply hearing sounds and not hearing words in one's own language. The set of features of the world recognised as a morally relevant element is recognised as a symbol. This is what is functioning as a symbol in M&PM.

Moral agents and moral patients are two examples from more established moral terminology that serve to illustrate the idea of morally relevant elements.[4] So, within a particular intuitive morality, it would be impossible not to see a particular entity as a moral patient, say, if that particular entity were recognised as such. But importantly, human moral agents and human moral patients are not the only two morally relevant elements possibly in play. The fact that different intuitive moralities may or may not see particular human institutions (e.g. corporations) as moral agents or individual animals within particular species of animals (e.g. chickens or pigs) as moral patients, say, serves to illustrate the fact that different intuitive moralities recognise different features of the world as morally relevant elements.

There is a danger here of missing an important point about LAMP (and M&PM). The analogy with language assumes there is a *distinct subject matter but similar* structure that is why the analogy is useful. Thus, there is a moral language distinct from linguistic language. So, to use linguistic language to refer to morally relevant elements is not to use moral language itself, but to use linguistic language to talk about another language, namely a moral language. Moral philosophers have used linguistic language to talk about morality, but they may have overlooked the possibility that moral language is a different language independent from linguistic language.[5] It is like using the sense of sight to describe the sense of smell.

So, just as humans have learnt to hear their native language in what to other humans (who have learnt a different language) are just meaningless sounds, humans have also learnt to intuit their native morality (they intuit morally relevant elements) in what to other humans (who have learnt a different intuitive morality) are just features of experience with no moral relevance. Importantly, of course, many morally relevant elements may be shared by different intuitive moralities (that is why there are commonalities between human intuitive moralities). But, also importantly, not all the details of each intuitive morality need be shared (that is why there are differences between human intuitive moralities).

Indeed, this is one of the most powerful reasons to accept LAMP/ M&PM as a scientific research programme seeking to understand moral intuitions. And just as a human who is competent in their native language can construct and comprehend the elements (words and grammatical sentences) of their native language with ease, so too a human who is competent in their intuitive morality can construct and comprehend the morally relevant elements of their intuitive morality.

## Mords, mentences, and moral meaning: moral syntax and semantics

The following set of pairs of claims is at the heart of LAMP/M&PM. This set of pairs is my attempt to re-frame the analogy in a way that will help orientate future research in the area. The first of each set refers to a linguistic capacity, and the second refers to a moral capacity.

Humans with the relevant capacity (either linguistic or moralistic) are capable of:

1L  Apprehending a state of affairs as containing linguistically relevant elements.

1M Apprehending a state of affairs as containing morally relevant elements.

2L  Apprehending a word as an element of a sentence.

2M Apprehending a mord as an element of a mentence.

3L  Apprehending a sentence as grammatical or ungrammatical.

3M Apprehending a mentence as morally well formed, or not morally well formed.(By analogy, 'not morally well formed' mentences are 'not morally grammatical.')

4L  Apprehending the meaning of a grammatical sentence.

4M Apprehending the moral meaning of a morally well-formed mentence.

But importantly, in comparison to linguistic meanings, there are very few moral meanings; they include (but presumably are not limited to): 'obligatory' and 'impermissible' (understood in the moral sense of these terms). At this point, it is worth acknowledging the distinction between grammar and categorisation. Roedder and Harman (2010, 280) note that many moral judgements are categorisations of an action, person, or situation. My suggestion, that there are very few moral meanings, could be understood as a claim about categorisation into one of very few categories rather than a claim about there being very few moral meanings. The categorisation approach has been explored by Stich (1993). Whether 'moral meanings' or 'moral categories' is the best way to understand the object of my analysis in this book is a question for the future.

Now to explain some of these claims. In relation to (1L), linguistic elements are sentences, and words (smaller linguistic units are ignored in this analysis). Suitably arranged words make up sentences (2L & 3L). But note that words can be arranged such that they don't make up a (grammatical) sentence (also 3L). In relation to (1M), moral elements are elements of a situation that correspond analogously to sentences, and words. Here, I call them 'mords' and 'mentences.' So, suitably arranged mords make up mentences (2M & 3M). But note that mords can be arranged such that they don't make up a (morally well-formed) mentence (also 3M).

Perhaps, mords and mentences can be represented in language with words and sentences, but very importantly, I assume they exist independently from language (hence 4L & 4M). That is the whole point of the linguistic *analogy* in moral psychology. Within M&PM, the moral faculty is assumed to be *distinct* from the language faculty. I suspect that the moral faculty is an evolutionary precursor to the language faculty, but whether or not this is the case, I assume they are distinct faculties.[6] Mords and mentences are the building blocks of intuitive morality, just as words and sentences are the building blocks of natural language. So, it is possible that there are mords and mentences that cannot easily be represented by words and sentences. I suggest this is why moral intuitions, sometimes, cannot be easily articulated in language.[7]

The word 'agent' in English can be used by the language faculty in sentences about agents. But, I claim, the word 'agent' as used by the language faculty is distinct from the intuitive concept *agent* that is central to the functioning of Spelke and Kinzler's agent core knowledge system (2007). Similarly, mords, such as the mord that is (perhaps imperfectly) referred to by the word 'kill' has a moral meaning distinct from the linguistic meaning of the word 'kill' as it is used in natural language. And again, this is why moral intuitions about killing may not be easily articulated in language.

Hopefully, an example will help illustrate the distinction between the language faculty and its use of words and sentences, and the moral faculty and its use of mords and mentences. Consider the experiment conducted by Heider and Simmel (1944) in which experimental subjects were asked to watch a short film and interpret/describe a number of geometric figures (two triangles of slightly different sizes and one circle approximately the same size as the smaller triangle), and their movements, in and around a larger rectangular shape (with part of the rectangular shape allowing the geometric figures to move in and out of the area bounded by that shape).[8] The vast majority of subjects interpreted or described the figures and their movements as persons moving in and around a building accessed via a door. I assume this is because the agent core knowledge system identified by Spelke and Kinzler is generating the output that characterises these movements as the movements of agents (persons). More importantly, for present purposes, not only did subjects describe the movements as movements of persons, but the descriptions included moral judgements. For example, the larger triangle was described by a number of subjects as a bully and/or a villain. So, I suggest that the moral faculty (narrow) is generating moral intuitions downstream of the agent core knowledge system – both of these operating within the moral faculty (broad) – and only after the fact is the language faculty of the experimental subjects reporting (perhaps only approximately) in language the outputs of both their agent core knowledge system and their moral faculty.

Reinterpreting the experiment of Heider and Simmel using mords and mentences, experimental subjects watching the movements of the geometric figures see the figures as agents and then as their experience unfolds, the subjects see the whole scenario as made up of morally relevant elements in morally relevant contexts, namely, mords (a mord identifies an agent, for example, the larger triangle, as a villain) and mentences (a mentence identifies the villain as bullying the smaller triangle).

Furthermore, mords and mentences may or may not be arranged in morally well-formed ways (this is the equivalent of words and sentences either being arranged grammatically or ungrammatically). If a state of affairs is morally well-formed, then it will have a moral meaning. For example, it might be obligatory or impermissible. So, the meaning of the mentence "the villain is bullying the smaller triangle" might be 'impermissible.' But if a state of affairs is not morally well-formed, it won't have a moral meaning at all. It literally won't make sense to say that it is obligatory or impermissible in a moral sense because it is not morally well-formed.

Importantly, some people may disagree about whether or not a state of affairs is (1) morally well-formed and (2) what the morally meaning is of that morally well-formed mentence (for example, whether it is morally impermissible to intentionally destroy one's own property, when it affects no one else). But that is because they are 'speaking' different moral languages.

Consider again the experiment of Heider and Simmel. Early in the film, the larger triangle approaches and makes contact with the smaller triangle a number of times in quick succession. A person experiencing this set of events may apprehend a morally well-formed mentence. For example, I apprehend (from the perspective of my intuitive morality), a morally well-formed mentence. And, this is because it has morally relevant elements in a morally relevant context arranged in a way that yields a moral meaning. I suggest that experimental subjects viewing the film (if they hold a similar intuitive morality to me) would have experienced an intuitive moral judgement at this point (e.g. that the action of the larger triangle was impermissible). Contrast this with the end of the film at which time the smaller triangle and circle have disappeared from view and the larger triangle then approaches and makes contact with the larger rectangular shape and this movement results in the larger rectangular shape breaking up into smaller pieces. This, I assume for the purposes of making this contrast, is not a morally well-formed mentence, and this is because (again I am making an assumption here in order to make this point) it does not have morally relevant elements within a morally relevant context arranged in a way that yields moral meaning. I suggest that experimental subjects viewing the film would not have experienced an intuitive moral judgement at this point (e.g. they would not judge the action to be impermissible). Strictly speaking, experimental subjects *may* have experienced an intuitive moral judgement at this point, but this would be because some of the subjects would have apprehended a moral meaning in the set of circumstances (i.e. because they 'speak' a different moral language to me). The point of this contrast is that some will see a morally relevant difference between the scene early in the film and the scene at the end of the film, and the relevant difference some will see is that in the first scene an agent/patient is being *attacked* (and, hence, this is impermissible) and in the final scene no other agent/patient is present (and, hence, the action is not impermissible). Of course, some people may not see a relevant moral distinction between *attacking* another agent/patient and *damaging* inanimate objects, but for the purpose of this point, I am assuming that there is a morally relevant distinction. This relates to the point made above that people 'speak' different moral languages.

Before I go on, I want to emphasise the claim that there are very few moral meanings. There are many linguistic meanings of sentences, but there are very few moral meanings of mentences. The moral meanings of mentences include *obligatory* or *impermissible* (when these are interpreted in a moral sense). There may well be more moral meanings of mentences that I don't examine here (for example, 'good' or 'bad' when these are understood in their moral senses). So, one of the central tasks of the M&PM research programme will be to address this issue of how many moral meanings exist in moral languages.

To illustrate this issue another way, consider the fact that natural language allows for the same linguistic meaning to be represented by a number of distinct sentences in natural language (i.e. synonymous sentences). For example, consider the following two sentences. 'From my perspective the apple is to the right of the orange on the table.' And, 'The orange is to the left of the apple on the table from my perspective.' These two sentences have the same meaning, so the concept of synonymous sentences is an existing feature of natural language. But now, imagine that there are very many synonymous mentences. As a consequence, very many mentences will have the moral meaning 'obligatory,' or alternatively very many mentences will have the moral meaning 'impermissible.' If it is true that there are relatively few moral meanings of mentences, then this is one of the significant disanalogies between the human capacity for language and the human capacity for moral intuition. Disanalogies such as this might explain why relatively few researchers have seen the value of the analogy. Hopefully by making disanalogies explicit (and setting them aside), more researchers will see the useful scope of the analogy.

## What is the moralistic equivalent of pragmatics?

Pragmatics in linguistics is the study of language use. Harley (2014, 449) characterises pragmatics as 'concerned with how we get things done with language' and a simple analogical reconstrual yields a significant insight. In M&PM, pragmatics is concerned with how we get things done with moral intuitions. So how do we get things done with moral intuitions? This question is a simple version of Marr's questions at the computational level of the 'tri-level hypothesis': "What is the goal of the computation, why is it appropriate, and what is the logic of the strategy by which it can be carried out?" (1982, 25).[9]

All these questions cast intuitive moral categorisation in a revealing light. But to focus on answering the simple version: We get things done with moral intuitions by getting everyone in a social group who are seeking (either consciously or otherwise) to coordinate their action to come to see the same things as obligatory, or impermissible, etc. The capacity to experience moral intuitions evolved to facilitate effective coordination within a social group. Notice that the specific content of the moral intuitions is not central to this way of seeing intuitive moral categorisation. The important question is this: do a set of moral intuitions that are shared by individuals in a social group do a good job of facilitating coordinated behaviour? And importantly, as mentioned previously, this is 'coordinated behaviour' as understood in the broadest of terms.

This broad understanding of 'coordinated behaviour' is a confronting idea. Some types of coordinated behaviour (and hence intuitively moral behaviour), as seen from within one intuitive moral language, may be seen from within another intuitive moral language as immoral (because this other intuitive moral language is coordinating behaviour in a different way). Recall the examples of sexual morality and slavery discussed previously. But, of course, behaviour is only intuitively judged as moral or immoral from within an intuitive moral language.[9]

Consider the advice: 'lead, follow, or get out of the way.'[10] There are a number of ways individuals might lead, from what might be described as authoritarian leadership through consultative leadership, to 'servant leadership' (Greenleaf 2007). And there are a number of ways individuals might follow, that would complement, or fail to complement, authoritarian leadership though consultative leadership, to 'servant leadership.' If there is a mismatch between the expectations of what is to lead and what it is to follow, then coordination is not manifest. But if there is a match between the expectations of what it is to lead and what it is to follow, then coordination is manifest. It is the manifestation of social coordination that is central here, not any assumptions about what coordination should look like. Indeed, if there is a mismatch between the expectation of what 'leading' and 'following' should look like, the advice still holds, in that one or other party should get out of the way. In other words, one or other party should simply stop attempting to coordinate, unless one or other party is able to adjust their expectation of what it means to be in a coordinated relationship. Suitably aligned moral intuitions facilitate social coordination, or more colloquially, speaking the same moral language gets things done.

Consideration of Quine's analysis of what he calls the 'conceptual scheme of science' is helpful at this point. The point of the conceptual scheme of science, for Quine, is to predict the future in the light of past experience (1980b, 44). But importantly, Quine acknowledges that predicting the future is only one purpose among other possible 'interests and purposes' (1980a, 19) with which humans might concern themselves. This acknowledgement of Quine's prompted me to think about conceptual schemes more broadly (Wood 2017). Perhaps humans have evolved in such a way that they have the capacity to construct a number of conceptual schemes. One such scheme may have the purpose of predicting the future, but another may have the purpose of facilitating social coordination. And perhaps, the need for social coordination was sufficiently important in our evolutionary past that evolution produced a dedicated set of structures, systems, and processes within System 1 that generate conceptual schemes that facilitate social coordination (i.e. moral languages). I suggest that such structures, systems, and processes do exist and generate our moral intuitions, in a way analogous to the way our natural language is generated and comprehended.

One way of illustrating how pragmatics might be pursued in research within M&PM is to consider Austin's work on speech acts. Austin (1962, 101) identifies three types of speech act – Locution, Illocution, and Perlocution – and illustrates them as follows:

> "He said…" is an example of a Locution (i.e., the meaning of what was actually said).

"He urged..." is an example of an Illocution (i.e., what the speaker hoped to achieve). "He persuaded..." is an example of a Perlocution (i.e., what was actually achieved).

(1962, 101)

Harley (2014, 450), describing the work of Austin, characterises the Locutionary Force of a sentence as the literal meaning of a sentence, the Illocutionary Force as what the speaker is trying to achieve, and the Perlocutionary Force as the actual effect on the listener.

Three analogous forces can be identified in Moralistics, namely, the Moralising Force, the Comoralising Force, and the Remoralising Force. But importantly, these forces do not relate to sentences but rather to mentences (i.e. morally well-formed morally relevant elements within morally relevant contexts that have moral meanings).

The Moralising Force relates to the literal moral meaning of the mentence. Thus, the morally well-formed mentence might mean *obligatory* or *impermissible*.

The Comoralising Force relates to what the person endorsing the mentence is trying to achieve, namely, getting other people to endorse the same mentence in the same way. In other words, the endorser of the mentences might see some states of affairs as *impermissible* and associated with that act of seeing things that way is another act of urging others to see things that way too. Indeed, implicit in moralising is the attempt to get others to see the morally relevant elements arranged in the same way as the moraliser sees them.

The Remoralising Force relates to the actual effect on others. If the Comoralising Force is successful, then others subject to the Comoralising Force will come to endorse the mentence in the same way as does the original endorser. And the result is social coordination (assuming that all parties act in accord with their moral language, i.e. their performance corresponds to their competence in their moral language). But this may not be the case. The others, although the Comoralising Force was directed at them, may reject seeing some state of affairs as *impermissible* and see it as *permissible* say, or, indeed, may not apprehend it as morally well-formed at all. If this occurs, social coordination is less likely.

Now all of these dimensions of moralistic acts (analogous to speech acts) may be mediated through natural language (i.e. speech acts), but importantly, they may not be. Moralistic acts may be mediated through non-linguistic behaviour. This is because the moral faculty is distinct from the language faculty, or so I assume.

## Illustrating the re-framed linguistic analogy

Having presented the re-framed linguistic analogy, I now present an example. I will use a suggestion made by Harman (2008) to illustrate how it may be operating within intuitive moral categorisations and describe that illustration in terms of moral syntax, moral semantics, mords, and mentences.

Harman (2008, 347) suggests that "there might be a universal principle containing a parameter G forbidding harm to members of G, where different moralities have different specifications of the relevant G." So, now, I consider Harman's suggestion using the conceptual resources of moral syntax, moral semantics, mords, and mentences.

Consider the mentence: 'X harms a member of G.'

First consider moral semantics. Let us stipulate for the purposes of this example that the moral meaning of "X harms a member of G" is *impermissible*. Notice that the sentence in natural language "It is impermissible that X harms a member of G" is a combination of the mentence and its moral meaning.[11]

Now, consider the possibility that the mentence "X harms a member of G" might have a different moral meaning. It might mean *permissible* rather than *impermissible*. Importantly, this is not the suggestion that Harman makes, but the conceptual resources within M&PM may allow for this possibility. Again notice that the sentence "It is permissible that X harms a member of G." is a combination of a mentence and this different moral meaning. Importantly, the mentence "X harms a member of G" cannot mean both 'impermissible' and 'permissible' for the same G in the same moral language. So, these two moral meanings exist in different moral languages.[12]

Now, consider moral syntax. To examine the moral syntax of the mentence 'X harms a member of G,' we must consider the individuals that are the actual instantiations of both 'X' and 'member of G' (I will refer to each possible individual instantiation of X as 'x' and each possible member of G as 'g'). Here, I am assuming the individual instantiating X is a moral agent in the traditional sense of this term.[13] To highlight the significance of this assumption, consider the implication if the individual that was instantiating X in some circumstance was not a moral agent (call this non-moral agent 'x*'). Then, the mentence 'X harms a member of G' becomes morally ungrammatical, because x* is not a moral agent, so the meaning of 'X harms a member of G' ceases to be *impermissible*, simply because entities that are not moral agents cannot be the subject of such a mentence.

Now consider the actual individual 'g' who is purported to be a 'member of G.' If the actual individual 'g,' purported to be a member of G, is a member of G, then the meaning of the mentence 'X harms g' is *impermissible*. However, if the actual individual (call this individual 'g\*'), purported to be a member of G, is not a member of G, then the meaning of the mentence 'X harms g\*' is not *impermissible*. This is because g\* is not a member of G.

Finally, let us consider the question of whether or not some action is deemed to be a harm within a moral language. If some action is deemed to be a harm, then the fact that the moral meaning of 'X harms a member of G' is *impermissible* is applicable to the consideration of this action. But if some action is not deemed to be a harm within a moral language, then the moral meaning of 'X harms a member of G' as *impermissible* is not applicable to that action because it is not deemed to be a harm. Figure 3.1 represents the computation generating intuitions corresponding to Harman's proposed principle prohibiting harming members of G, and in this flowchart, it is assumed that X is a moral agent.

I think Harman's suggestion that there exists a universal moral principle that prohibits harming members of G (where membership of G varies relative to different moral languages) is a good one. Harman's principle can be enriched by a further suggestion that different moral languages may have different intuitive assumptions (possibly instantiated as different parameter settings) about what types of actions constitute harms. And recall that Mikhail (2011) is seeking to identify the computational moral grammar underlying intuitive 'permissible' and 'impermissible' judgements of harm in trolley car cases.

Throughout my analysis, I have focused on the moral meanings of 'impermissible' and 'obligatory.' But as I have noted, there may be other moral meanings, such as 'good' or 'bad' (where these are understood in their moral senses). So here is brief example involving 'morally good' and 'morally bad.' And this example has the added value of indicating how Nietzsche's insights into moral psychology (as presented by Leiter) can be understood within the framework of M&PM. Leiter (2019) points to Nietzsche's discussion of cowardice and humility in *Daybreak* that illustrates different attitudes the ancient Greeks and Christian had to the same disposition, namely, a "disposition to avoid offending dangerous enemies" (2019, 75). The ancient Greeks had a negative attitude to those who manifest this disposition, recognising it as cowardice, while the Christians had a positive attitude to those who manifest it, recognising it as humility. Leiter characterises

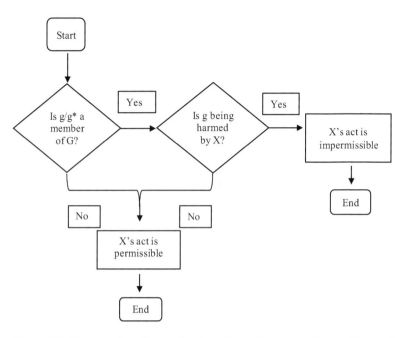

*Figure 3.1* Computation Generating Intuitions Corresponding to Harman's
Principle.

all of this in terms of affect, but, of course, I am interested in what
triggered the affect. So, here is an alternative characterisation in terms
of the re-framed linguistic analogy. The disposition 'avoid offending
dangerous enemies' is the mentence and the meaning of that mentence
in the moral language of the ancient Greeks is *morally bad* and the
meaning of the mentence in the moral language of the Christians is
*morally good*. Hence, the ancient Greeks interpret it is as cowardice
and the Christians interpret it as humility.

I claim that moral principles such as the one suggested by Harman
and examined in detail here are a core part of the production of moral
intuitions, as they were imagined by Rawls, such that the total set of
such principles constitute the universal moral grammar as described
by Mikhail (2007). The actual moral grammar of any individual
human would be the result of the parameters within the principles taking on certain values (presumably through a process of socialisation)
such that the principles can function in computations. The outputs of
these computations are experienced by individual humans as moral
intuitions.

**Summary of chapter and a concluding remark**

In this chapter, I have described how I imagine the scientific research programme of M&PM might proceed. I suggest (1) identifying a feature of linguistics and/or psycholinguistics, (2) assume an analogical feature exists in Moralistics and/or Psychomoralitics, and then (3) test whether or not that feature exists. Assuming what I have suggested here is on the right track, there is still obviously a great deal of future work to be done to identify the nature and structure of the relevant structures, systems, and processes generating intuitive moral categorisations. But Rawls was aware of this when he said:

> Only a deceptive familiarity with our everyday judgments and our natural readiness to make them could conceal the fact that characterising our moral capacities is an intricate task. The principles which describe them must be presumed to have a complex structure, and the concepts involved will require serious study.
>
> (1973, 46)

To give some sense of the possible future direction of the research programme, Table 3.2 lists not only questions I have addressed in this book but also further possible questions. I stress that these are only possible questions because one central task of the research programme is to uncover how far the analogy between linguistics and moral intuitions extends. Analogies as well as disanalogies will be found. Another central task of the research programme will be to understand its 'core claims.' Lakatos understood scientific research programmes to have both "hard core" claims and "auxiliary hypotheses" (1974, 100). One of the tasks of researchers in the M&PM research programme will be to reflect on this distinction. Auxiliary assumptions can change, but if the 'hard core' claims of the research programme are relinquished then, according to Lakatos, the research programme itself has been relinquished.

I am suggesting a significant re-framing of the LAMP scientific research programme, in which I offer a unification of LAMP, MFT, and CASE. I accept that what I have proposed here is a bold set of conjectures. In the spirit of Popperian science, I am open to the refutation of these conjectures (Popper 1974). But, more optimistically, and following Lakatos (1968), rather than Popper, I invite others to help move (what might be called a little harshly) the currently degenerating research programme, known as the Linguistic Analogy in Moral Psychology, toward a progressive scientific research programme that I call Moralistics and Psychomoralistics: a unified cognitive science of moral intuition.

*Table 3.2* Possible research questions in Moralistics and Psychomoralistics

| Linguistic Terms | Questions About Equivalent Moralistic Terms |
| --- | --- |
| Language | What is the moralistic equivalent of language? |
| Words | What is the moralistic equivalent of words (call them 'mords')? |
| Sentences | What is the moralistic equivalent of sentences (call them 'mentences')? |
| Syntax | What is the moralistic equivalent of syntax? |
| Semantics | What is the moralistic equivalent of semantics? |
| Pragmatics | What is the moralistic equivalent of pragmatics? |
| Morphology | What is the moralistic equivalent of morphology? |
| Inflectional morphology | What is the moralistic equivalent of inflectional morphology? |
| Derivational morphology | What is the moralistic equivalent of derivational morphology? |
| Phonetics | What is the moralistic equivalent of phonetics? |
| Phonology | What is the moralistic equivalent of phonology? |
| Broca's Aphasia | What is the moralistic equivalent of Broca's Aphasia? |
| Wernicke's Aphasia | What is the moralistic equivalent of Wernicke's Aphasia? |
| Dyslexia | What is the moralistic equivalent of dyslexia? |

## Notes

1 With reference to any particular empirical test, or series of empirical tests, the actual process might involve a null hypothesis that some cognitive structure or process does not exist, and then would involve tests that may or may not lead to the rejection of the null hypothesis.
2 Another assumption in the set of 'hard core' claims (using Lakatos's language) in the M&PM research programme (as I understand it) is that intuitive moral categorisation evolved due to its biological function in furthering social coordination among social mammals.
3 There is another parallel here with Dennett's concept of 'real patterns' but again space limitations preclude further analysis (1991).
4 Without getting into a more involved discussion that is not necessary in the current context, moral agents have a responsibility to act morally and moral patients have a right to be treated morally.
5 Wittgenstein did not go so far as to say that there was distinct moral language, but he did think that morality (or as he would say ethics) could not be articulated in language (1965).
6 In biology there is a distinction drawn between homologous and analogous structures within organisms. Homologous structures share a common

evolutionary origin, while analogous structures function in similar ways (independently from whether or not they share a common evolutionary origin). If my suggestion that the moral faculty is an evolutionary precursor to the language faculty then to the extent that both faculties involve a grammar then presumably they are homologues and analogues of each other.

7 Again, I think that Wittgenstein's thoughts on ethics are relevant here (1965).

8 If you are unfamiliar with this research I encourage you to stop reading and watch this video which is readily available online.

9 Moral relativism (Gowans 2021) would be relevant to discuss at this point, if this book was principally concerned with moral philosophy as opposed to moral psychology, but this is a descriptive project, not a normative project.

10 Another saying that could be analysed in the same way as this one is: "Do not walk in front of me, I may not follow. Do not walk behind me, I may not lead. Walk beside me and be my friend." (Attribution unknown)

11 There is an interesting parallel between "It is impermissible that ..." and "It is false that ..." I assume there is something interesting to be said here, but that will have to wait for another time.

12 There is a complication here whereby the set of moral computations might involve a number of mentences that combine together and only the computation taken together as a whole has an overall moral meaning of permissible or impermissible. But this level of analysis will have to wait for further progress within the M&PM research programme.

13 Again, without getting into a more involved discussion that is not necessary in the current context, moral agents have a responsibility to act morally and moral patients have a right to be treated morally.

## References

Austin, J. L. 1962. *How To Do Things with Words*. Oxford: Clarendon Press.

Dennett, Daniel. 1991. "Real Patterns." *The Journal of Philosophy* 88 (1):27–51.

Dwyer, Susan, Bryce Huebner, and Marc D. Hauser. 2010. "The Linguistic Analogy: Motivations, Results, and Speculations." *Topics in Cognitive Science* 2:486–510.

Fodor, Jerry. 1983. *The Modularity of Mind*. Cambridge: MIT.

Gowans, Chris. 2021. "Moral Relativism." In *The Stanford Encyclopedia of Philosophy*, edited by Edward Zalta. Stanford, CA: Metaphysics Research Lab, Stanford University, https://plato.stanford.edu/entries/moral-relativism/

Greenleaf, Robert. 2007. "The Servant as Leader." In *Corporate Ethics and Corporate Governance*, edited by Walther Zimmerli, Klaus Richter and Markus Holzinger, 79–86. Berlin: Springer.

Harley, Trevor. 2014. *The Psychology of Language: From Data to Theory*. New York: Psychology Press.

Harman, Gilbert H. 2008. "Using a Linguistic Analogy to Study Morality." In *Moral Psychology Volume 1: The Evolution of Morality: Adaptations and*

*Innateness*, edited by Walter Sinnott-Armstrong, 345–352. Cambridge MA: MIT Press.

Heider, F., and M. Simmel. 1944. "An Experimental Study of Apparent Behavior." *The American Journal of Psychology* 57 (2): 243–259.

Kahneman, Daniel. 2002. *Nobel Prize Lecture - Maps of Bounded Rationality: A Perspective on Intuitive Judgment and Choice.* Sweden: The Nobel Foundation, https://www.nobelprize.org/uploads/2018/06/kahnemann-lecture.pdf

Lakatos, Imre. 1968. "Criticism and Methodology of Scientific Research Programmes." *Proceedings of the Aristotelian Society* 69:149–186.

Lakatos, Imre. 1974. "Science and Pseudoscience." In *Philosophy in the Open*, edited by G Vessey, 96–102. London: Open University Press.

Leiter, Brian. 2019. *Moral Psychology with Nietzsche.* Oxford: Oxford University Press.

Marr, David. 1982. *Vision: A Computational Investigation into the Human Representation and Processing of Visual Information.* San Francisco, CA: W. H. Freeman.

Mikhail, John. 2007. "Universal Moral Grammar: Theory, Evidence, and the Future." *Trends in Cognitive Science* 11 (4):143–152.

Mikhail, John. 2011. *Elements of Moral Cognition: Rawl's Linguistic Analogy and the Cognitive Science of Moral and Legal Judgment.* Cambridge: Cambridge University Press.

Popper, Karl. 1974. *Conjectures and Refutations: The Growth of Scientific Knowledge.* Oxford: Routledge.

Quine, W. V. 1980a. "On What There Is." In *From a Logical Point of View*, 1-19, Cambridge MA: Harvard University Press.

Quine, W. V. 1980b. "Two Dogmas of Empiricism." In *From a Logical Point of View*, 20–46. Cambridge, MA: Harvard University Press.

Rawls, John. 1973. *A Theory of Justice.* Oxford: Oxford University Press.

Roedder, Erica, and Gilbert H. Harman. 2010. "Linguistics and Moral Theory." In *The Moral Psychology Handbook*, edited by John Doris, 273–296. Oxford: Oxford University Press.

Saunders, Leland F. 2009. "Reason and Intuition in the Moral Life: A Dual-Process Account of Moral Justification." In Jonathan St. B. T. Evans and Keith Frankish (eds) *In Two Minds: Dual Processes and beyond*, 335–354. Oxford: Oxford University Press.

Stich, Stephen. 1993. "Moral Philosophy and Mental Representation." In *The Origins of Values*, edited by M. Hechter, L. Nadel and R. Michod, 215–228. New York: Aldine de Gruyter.

Wittgenstein, L. 1965. "A Lecture on Ethics." *The Philosophical Review* 74 (1): 3–12.

Wood, Graham. 2017. "Do Religious Beliefs Have a Place Within an 'Epistemically Naturalised' Cognitive System?" *Sophia* 56 (4):539–556.

# Index

Note: **Bold** page numbers refer to tables; *italic* page numbers refer to figures and page numbers followed by "n" denote endnotes.

act tree 33, 57
adaptive problem 7–8, 12
algorithm 15–18, 30, 33, 36–39
analogical reconstrual 59, 65
apparent behaviour *see* experiments
archery 20
Aristotle *see* slavery
Austin, J. L. 66–67; *see also* speech acts
automatic/automaticity 5, 14, 35, 56

Baumeister, Roy F. *see* sex
biological function 42–43, 72n2
biologically evolved system/faculty 2, 4, 29, 43
blank slate 8
Brown *see* human universals
Buss, David M. 48

Cartesian Theatre 9
categorisation 2–7, 16, 18, 61
cheating 36–39, *40*
Chomsky, Noam 31–32
Code of Hammurabi 24n1, 48; *see also* slavery
Cognitive Adaptations for Social Exchange (CASE) 2–3, 36–39
cognitive science *see* tri-level hypothesis
cognitive system: deep and distinct 8–10, 13; multi-level 12–13
communication 8–11, 17, 30, 58
compassion 2, 5

competence/performance 32–33, 39–41, 67
computation 15–18, 30–33, 36, 57, 69, *70*
confound 22, 33
conjecture 71
consciousness 9–12, 34
contract *see* Cognitive Adaptations for Social Exchange
core knowledge system 11, 13, 18, 62
Cosmides, Leda 12, 36, 47–48; *see also* Cognitive Adaptations for Social Exchange; rationed benefit
cowardice 69–70

Dennett, Daniel 10, 34; *see also* Cartesian Theatre; design space; Pandemonium; real patterns
design space 9, 17
disanalogy 50n4, 64–65, 71
doctrine of double effect 33, 36, 40
domain (proper/actual) 42–43
dual-system theory 13; *see also* systems
Dwyer, Susan 56–57; *see also* Linguistic Analogy in Moral Psychology

elephant 1–2, 29, 55
emotion 7, 20, 38, 46
Environment of Evolutionary Adaptedness (EEA) 8
Evans, Jonathan St. B. T. 14

evolutionary analysis 7–9, 45
evolutionary change 2
evolutionary pressure 8–10, 16–18
evolutionary psychology 8, 24, 36
examples 30–31, 35, 44–46, 49–50, 65
experiments: apparent behaviour
  62–64; Julie and Mark 35, 45;
  trolley car 33, 57, 69

fairness 36–39, *40*
Fodor, Jerry 12–13, 18, 59; *see also*
  mandatoriness
forbidding harm to members of G
  32, 49, 68
Force (Moralising, Comoralising,
  Remoralising) 67
framework for the psychology of
  norms 3, 41–43
Frankish, Keith 14

Graham, Jesse *see* Moral
  Foundations Theory
grammar 2, 31, 33, 61, 70

Haidt, Jonathan 34–35, 45; *see also*
  Moral Foundations Theory
Hammurabi 24n1, 48; *see also*
  slavery
hard cases 50
Harley, Trevor 58, 65; *see also*
  linguistics
harm 32, *40*, 69
Harman, Gilbert H. 45, 49, 68–70;
  *see also* forbidding harm to
  members of G; hard cases
Hauser, Marc D. 17–19, 56–57; *see
  also* moral faculty (narrow/broad)
Heider, F. 62–64; *see* also experiment
  (apparent behaviour)
hierarchy 30, 45
history 2, 4, 31, 44–45
Huebner, Bryce 56–57; *see also*
  emotion
human universals 19
humility 69–70

i-grammar 25n20, 50n1
information-processing 15, 29, 43
introspection 7, 9–11
intuitionism 35

Johnson, Mark 19; *see also* moral
  faculty (denial of)
justice 2, 5; *see also* sense of justice
justification 35, 44–45, 48

Kahneman, Daniel 14, 56
Kinzler, Katherine 11; *see also* core
  knowledge systems
Kohlberg, Lawrence 34

Lakatos, Imre 55, 57, 71, 72n2
language: competence 33, 39–41;
  faculty 17–19, 21, *39*; moral 40–45,
  60, 65–70; natural 2, 19, 39, 59
leadership 65–66
Leiter, Brian *see* Nietzsche
Linguistic Analogy in Moral
  Psychology (LAMP) 2–3, 17–19,
  31–34; disanalogies 64–65,
  71; distinct subject matter 60;
  principles and parameters *40*;
  re-framing of 55
linguistics: pragmatics 65–66;
  principles and parameters model
  (PPM) 31–33, *39*

Mackie, J. L. 6, 16, 21; *see also* not-
  to-be-doneness; ordinary moral
  judgements
mandatoriness 12, 59
Marr, David 15–18, 29, 65; *see also*
  tri-level hypothesis
marriage 48
McIlwain, James T. 9; *see* also
  photoreceptors
meaning: linguistic 61–62, 64; moral
  16, 60–64, 67–69
mentence 2, 60–64, 67–70, **72**
metaethics 4
Mikhail, John 33, 36, 40, 49, 57; *see
  also* Linguistic Analogy in Moral
  Psychology
Mill 1, 5–7
mind: dual-system/process theory of
  13; tripartite division (Stanovich)
  24n8; tripartite soul (Plato) 13
modularity 12–13, 43; criticism of
  massive modularity theory 24n5
moral (concept of) 21
moral agent/patient 59–60, 64, 68

moral authority 4
moral context 20, 23
moral/conventional distinction 42–43
moral deliberation 29, 35, 44
moral dumbfounding 35, 44
moral faculty 18–19, 22–23; broad/
    narrow 17–19, 62; constraints
    on 19; denial of existence of
    19; distinct from language
    faculty 62
Moral Foundations Theory (MFT)
    2–3, 34–35
moral intuition 3–7, 14–16, 20–22,
    29–35; how we get things do with
    65; not easily articulated in language
    62; *see also* Wittgenstein, L.
moral judgement (ordinary) 6–7
moral meaning 60–64
moral philosophy 44
moral psychology: descriptive 4, 22;
    nativism 35; pluralism 35
moral reasoning 2, 49, 56
Moralistics and Psychomoralistics
    (M&PM)1–3, 20, 55; assumptions
    3; implications 3–4; methodology
    58; possible research questions
    **72**; principles and parameters
    *40*; questions relating to possible
    analogies **58**; theoretical
    framework 2
morality: ability to use 21; concept
    of 21; customary 5–7, 16; ordinary
    6–7; rationality of 44
morally meaningful 18, 20–21
morally relevant elements/contexts
    2–3, 42, 55, 59–61, 63–64, 67
mords 2, 55, **58**, 60–63, 68, **72**
Müller-Lyer Ilusion 12, *13*

nativism 35
neuroscience 17, 19, 36
Nietzsche 69
normative ethics 4
normativity 22–23
norms *see* framework for the
    psychology of norms
not-to-be-doneness 6, 16

paired questions/claims 23, 60–61
Pandemonium 10, 34

performance/competence 32–33,
    *39–40*, 67
photoreceptors 9–11
Plato 13, 24n6
politics (US liberal/conservative
    distinction) 34
Popper, Karl 71
pornography 50n5
pragmatics **58**, 65–66, **72**; *see also*
    linguistics
prediction 8, 10, 11, 66
prescriptive force 5
principles and parameter settings in
    moral grammar 33, 38–*40*, 47, 50
Principles and Parameters Model
    (PPM) *see* Linguistic Analogy in
    Moral Psychology; linguistics
psycholinguistics 3, 17, 55, 58, 71
psychological phenomenon 5–7
psychology of norms *see* framework
    for the psychology of norms
Pylyshyn, Zenon 15–16; *see also* tri-
    level hypothesis

Quine, W. V. 66; *see also* conceptual
    scheme; prediction

rationed benefit 36–40, 45–48, 51n5
Rawls, John 6–7, 14, 31, 55–56, 71;
    *see also* Linguistic Analogy in
    Moral Psychology
real patterns 25n14, 72n3
reasoning 2, 14, 35, 49, 56
reflective equilibrium 56
reproductive potential and investment
    46–48
reproductive success 8, 43
research program 1–3, 29, 55, 57, 71,
    **72**, 72n2
Roedder, Erica *see* categorisation;
    i-grammar

Samuels, Richard 7–8; *see also*
    evolutionary analysis
Saunders, Leland F. 3, 29, 43–44, 56;
    *see also* moral dumbfounding
science (conceptual scheme of) 66
scientific research program
    (progressive) 55, 71
semantics 16, **58**, 60, 68, **72**

sense of justice 6–7, 14, 31, 55–56
sex 30; before marriage
   (impermissibility of) 48; cultural
   suppression of female sexuality
   48; female mate choice 46; incest
   35, 45–46; sexual economics
   46–47
sexual selection 46–47
should claims 22–23
Simmel, M. *see* apparent behaviour;
   experiment
slavery 4, 16, 31, 48–49; natural
   slaves 49
social contract algorithm 36–37;
   *see also* Cognitive Adaptations for
   Social Exchange
social cooperation 15–16
social coordination 8, 10–11, 15–16,
   30, 66–67
social mammals 8, 72n2
social norms *see* framework for the
   psychology of norms
social science (standard model) 8
socialisation 70
speech acts 66–67
Spelke, Elizabeth 11; *see also* core
   knowledge systems
Sperber, Dan 42–43
Spinoza, Baruch 4
Sripada, Chandra Sekhar 41–42;
   *see also* frameworks for the
   psychology of norms
Stanovich, Keith E. 14, 24n8; *see also*
   dual-system theory; system

Stich, Stephen 41–42; *see also*
   frameworks for the psychology of
   norms
structural descriptions 33, 57
symbols 15, 58–59
synonymous sentences 64
syntax 15–16, **58**, 60, 68, **72**
systems: (1 & 2) 14, 21, 29, 44–45, 56,
   66; core knowledge 11 13, 18, 62;
   dual 13

to-be-pursuedness 6, 16, 21
Tooby, John 12, 36, 47–48; *see also*
   Cognitive Adaptations for Social
   Exchange
tri-level hypothesis 15–16, 20, 33, 65;
   physical implementation of 16
trolley car *see* experiments
Turiel, Elliot *see* moral/conventional
   distinction

understanding 22, 25n16, 29
universal moral grammar *40*, 70
universal moral norms 19
universalisability 34

vision 9

Wason selection task 37
WEIRD (Western, Educated,
   Industrialised, Rich, Democratic) 42
West 14; *see also* systems (1 & 2)
Westermarck Mechanism 30, 46
Wittgenstein, L. 72n5, 73n7